✳ *Cook Until Done* ✳

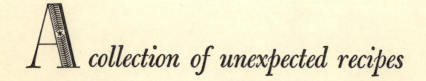
A collection of unexpected recipes

M. BARROWS AND COMPANY

✳

NEW YORK

COOK

* *Until Done*

*

George Bradshaw &
Ruth Norman

If there are too many "I's" in this book for a collaboration, blame me; I wrote it. But make no mistake about who the expert is: Ruth Norman.

G.B.

Contents

* 1 *

SOUFFLÉS

*

The first thing I ever cooked was an enormous success. It had, I'll admit, an impromptu quality about it, but that doesn't matter; the dish was a steak, and I will now put down the recipe as accurately as I can.

I was in California, living in one of those furnished apartments which had a kitchen stocked with enough pots and pans, dishes and silverware to serve a party of twelve. Until my moment of truth, I had not used this kitchen much—it was a place I went for ice. I was simply aware that, like the broom closet, it existed.

But then a girl I knew sent me a steak from Kansas City.

It was a pretty thing. Even my unaccustomed eye could see that it was a cut of a great animal: four inches thick, a sirloin, enormous, it was ostentatiously marbleized.

Just what decided me to cook it myself, I do not remember—probably a pitcher of martinis. In any case the decision was made, and I called up a couple of friends to come around and share my luck.

When we were hungry, about eight o'clock, I began. The oven was good and hot, for I had had the chambermaid light it at five, when she went off duty.

So. I opened the door of the broiler and put the steak under the gas. I then went into the living room and had a cigarette, or part of one. This would take, I should think, about three minutes. I then went back to the kitchen. The entire place was in flames.

Now here is where my recipe becomes a little inexact. I do not know *precisely* how long that kitchen was on fire. I did not look at my watch.

But I do know that when things had quieted down enough for me to get the broiler door open, the steak was perfectly done. Charred black on the outside, red rare on the inside, I have never tasted a better.

I suppose the fact that painters had to be called in the next day to fix up the kitchen does not properly belong in a recipe, but it is something to consider if you are contemplating broiling a steak.

I am not one of those fortunate people who has quivering memories of food eaten in childhood. I haven't the faintest idea what I ate or how it was prepared. In fact,

I was fifteen before it occurred to me that food wasn't something indigenous to a dining-room table.

When I was fifteen I went to a camp in Canada. I made friends with the chef there, a thin elegant old man in his seventies who shuffled around his kitchen in bedroom slippers, a homemade cigarette drooping constantly from beneath his drooping white mustache. I suppose he was some sort of failure, because he lived only to read; George Borrow was his favorite author. At his insistence that summer I got through both *Lavengro* and *Romany Rye*.

It was Chef who told me the first recipe I ever heard. We were sitting around his warm kitchen one night, the cold August rain dripping off the Canadian pines, he was remembering for me the fifty years he had spent cooking for carnivals and circuses, and quite naturally in his rambles the recipe came out.

It was a way to make tomato soup if you didn't have a can of tomato soup.

You put some milk in a pan, added a half teaspoon of soda, heated this, and then poured in a good shot of catsup.

This appeared to me to be a remarkable piece of information. I think I know why. It afforded me, of course, my first insight into the mystery of cooking, but it contained, as well, all the elements of a great recipe—imagination, economy, a basic knowledge of chemistry—all, possibly, except one: taste.

I repeated this recipe—smugly, I suppose—to anyone who would listen for the next couple of years. To my knowledge it was never made, certainly never by me, but

I pass it on for what it is worth, on the chance that someone will someday be desperate for a bowl of tomato soup.

That one episode, however, was the landmark of my
youth. From the time I was ten until I was twenty, I was
away at school and college, and whatever doors to virtue
our educational institutions open for us, the door to good
eating is not one of them. If I were forced to remember
those years they would reveal themselves as one long
session with tapioca.

No, meals then were simply another way to mark the
time of day, like an English precept or a geology class; the
thoughts of youth were presumably long, long thoughts,
but they were not on *ris de veau financière*.

I came, then, late to the table. I was twenty when my
uncle took me to dinner at Voisin, the celebrated New
York restaurant, and it was on that night that my fifth
sense was brought into play.

I was aware, almost immediately, of what was happen-
ing. I had had soup before. But this—was this soup, or
some miraculous accident that had occurred in the kitchen
and could never occur again? I had to decide no, for the
chicken, the salad, the French-fried parsley were all part
of the same miracle. I pretended of course, as you do at
twenty, that I had eaten before, and I don't think my
uncle detected that I wasn't my usual pretentious self
until the dessert.

"*What*," I said, "is this?"

Jules, the captain, said, "It's a chocolate soufflé. Do you
like it?"

Like it? Here was all glory in a two-quart bowl. Like it? I decided, with my mouth full, that I would probably have a soufflé every night for the rest of my life.

I wish things could have worked out that way. Circumstances, not to say money, decided otherwise. But at least I had had a beginning.

When I could afford it, of course, I bowled off to Voisin's and feasted. Jules became my friend and so did Aldo, his lieutenant. I sampled and resampled the long line of dessert soufflés: chocolate, almond, vanilla, lemon, and so on, and I felt I became knowing about sauces. But these times were special; on the ordinary day I just ate food—call it the mixture as before.

Also there was a setback in here. The war. Soufflés never entered my head for a good five years.

It wasn't, indeed, until my striking success with the steak that my personal interest in food began to revive. And something happened only three days later that was a real eye opener.

A girl I knew in Santa Monica asked me to lunch. She was a nice girl but an obvious scatterbrain and I imagined she would give me a fast tuna fish salad from the delicatessen with maybe a chocolate cupcake for dessert, but I went.

However, the very happy fact was that she produced from the kitchen a magnificent cheese soufflé. I jumped to the sensible conclusion that they were now flying soufflés out from New York, and that all you had to do was reheat them on arrival.

But I said politely, "My word. Did you make this yourself?"

She shrugged and said, "Certainly. Any fool can make a soufflé."

Any fool? I looked at her. This appeared to me to be too encouraging a statement to make about the end-product of French civilization.

"Is this a fact?" I said.

She nodded. "All you have to do is remember to let the sauce cool."

I shut up after that. I was in over my head. What sauce?

But I was hooked. On the way home I bought a flock of cookbooks. I told myself that I had, after all, learned how to take an automobile engine apart, and there was, therefore, no reason why I couldn't find out how to press a duck.

I spent an instructive evening among my books. The next day, after calling up a few people to find out what exactly was meant by a "tablespoon of flour," I set to work. At a quarter of four in the afternoon, I created my first soufflé. It was chocolate, it rose, and it was wonderful. I ate it all myself.

Well, so much for early success. With a little practice, I could make a soufflé that fell with the best of them. But I persisted, for I now realized that an ordinary, tax-paying, American citizen could make a soufflé, and that a ten-year apprenticeship in the licentious kitchens of Versailles was not, as I had supposed, necessary.

I have not, I am sorry to say, come upon an infallible

recipe. But I have learned a few tricks, the hard way. It is some trouble to make a soufflé, as it is some trouble to make anything that is any good. But if you will assume the posture of an artist and pay attention to the directions, You Too can make a soufflé.

Following are a good many recipes with some simple enough menus to go with them. Once you have learned how to make a soufflé, you will develop dreams of grandeur and think you must cook a whole meal.

FIRST, A FEW HINTS

Hear this: There is only one inflexible rule about a soufflé; it must be eaten when ready. A soufflé will not wait upon people: people must wait upon a soufflé.

You will benefit, I think, by reading the following paragraphs before you plunge into any of the recipes. They will give you some insight into *why* you are doing *what* you are doing—a very comfortable feeling for anyone who finds himself alone in a kitchen with his first soufflé.

Price: There seems to be some notion, probably because in restaurants they are, that soufflés are extremely expensive to make. This is nonsense. For a dessert soufflé, the ingredients probably won't add up to more than fifty or sixty cents, if that. You can't serve any other very gala dessert at fifteen cents a head.

The Soufflé Dish: You can make a soufflé in any heat-proof china casserole that has straight sides and holds approximately two quarts. It is good, however, to have the traditional French white china dish. It makes the soufflé look better when it comes to the table.

Don't try to double any of these recipes and make an enormous soufflé in an enormous dish. The batter will not cook through in the time allowed. If you need eight servings, make two soufflés of the usual size.

Preparation of the Dish: The soufflé dish should be rubbed with butter, bottom and sides. For entrée and vegetable soufflés, sprinkle a little flour over the butter. For dessert soufflés, sprinkle with a little sugar.

Oven: In all these recipes I say a 350° oven. It is probably true that if you turned every oven in the United States to 350° you would not get exactly the same temperature in any of them, so you have to try out yours. The soufflé must always be cooked in moderate heat. If the oven is too hot the soufflé will rise too quickly and the center will not cook at all. The oven must *always* be preheated.

You have to experiment. But *do not* overcook your soufflé.

Any recipe that tells you to leave your soufflé in the oven forty-five minutes or an hour, or an hour and a quarter, has been written by someone who has never had a soufflé.

Egg Whites: The whites of eggs should be beaten until they are stiff and creamy. They should not be overbeaten until they are hard and dry. If you use a hand beater you don't need to worry about this advice because you will probably be exhausted long before the whites are hard and dry.

But there is a reason for this warning for anyone who might be too ambitious with an electric mixer. If the whites are too stiff they simply will not combine easily and thoroughly with the sauce. So watch for the right moment, the whites will be ready when they glisten and stand in peaks.

In each one of the recipes you will notice that a large spoonful of whites is folded into the sauce *before* this sauce is dribbled into the remaining whites. *Don't* neglect to do this. It lightens the sauce—aerates it—so that you do not have the dead weight of a heavy mixture dropping— plunk—on the bubbles of egg whites.

Cooling: This is one of the real requirements of soufflé-making. The sauce must, no kidding, be cool.

A good way to determine this right temperature degree is to hold the top of your double boiler in the palm of your hand. If you can do this comfortably the sauce is cool.

On the other hand, none of the cooked sauces should ever be allowed to get completely cold.

Testing: A soufflé, as long as it remains in its warm oven, is a pretty sturdy dish. You don't have to worry about tip-toeing around the kitchen or opening the oven door to take a look. Indeed, I have found that the best way to determine whether a soufflé is done or not is to open the oven door at the end of eighteen or twenty minutes and give the dish a slight shove. If the top crust of the soufflé wiggles only very slightly, it is done. If, however, it really trembles, so that you have a feeling that there is nothing but soup underneath, let it go another few minutes.

Dessert soufflés should be softer than entrée or vegetable soufflés. The center of a great chocolate soufflé should be creamy and runny so that, in fact, if you have nothing else you can use this as a sauce for the crusty sides.

Servings: You can get no more than four portions from a soufflé. If the soufflé is a good one, three can easily eat it up. If you are hungry, two can do away with it, and one has been known . . .

ENTRÉE SOUFFLÉS
✳

CHEESE SOUFFLÉ

Melt 3 tablespoons of butter in the top of a double boiler. Mix in 3 tablespoons of flour. Cook a minute, then add one cup of milk and stir constantly until the sauce is thick and creamy. Now add one half pound of cheese. The cheese can be anything from Parmesan or Swiss to the sharpest kind of aged cheese; a good Cheddar should do to begin with.

The cheese should be cut into small pieces—the smaller, the easier for you—and then stirred into the mixture until it is entirely melted and you have a rich, thick, smooth sauce. Add a dash of cayenne pepper. Beat again, and set the top of the double boiler off its water to cool.

Separate six eggs. Beat the yolks and add them to the cheese mixture, and then beat again until all is genuinely combined. Allow this to cool. Really cool. Fifteen minutes.

Beat the egg whites (six) until they are stiff. Then take a large spoonful of them—almost a quarter of the whole—and mix thoroughly into the cheese sauce until you have a slightly foamy consistency. Now dribble this sauce over the remaining egg whites and fold and cut gently and firmly. Be a little timid with the first soufflé. If there are a few bits of unmixed egg white, never mind. Better too little than too much folding until you know what you are doing.

Now slide this whole thing into a buttered and floured soufflé dish and into a 350° oven.

It should take between twenty and twenty-five minutes to be done. But test it.

And have no fear. It will rise.

And there's your first. With thin slices of rye bread and a proper green salad you will have a meal worthy of your courage.

Many people are under the impression they can make a green salad. They buy a head of Iceberg lettuce and douse a bottle of Thousand Island dressing on it. This will not do. You must get decent lettuce: Boston, butter, bronze, Bibb, Belgian endive—a lettuce with a *taste*— you must wash it thoroughly leaf by leaf and then plunge it for half an hour into a bowl of iced water. You must dry it. Thoroughly. The thing to do is shake it and then spread it on a newspaper. I find *The New York Times* perfect. Turn it several times. Finally put it in a salad bowl and back into the icebox until it is cold. It must be cold.

(And there's only one way to make French dressing: As you make a rather poor martini—four to one: four olive oils to one tarragon vinegar, then enough salt and ground black pepper to suit you.)

HAMBURGER SOUFFLÉ

In the top of a double boiler melt 3 tablespoons of butter, add 3 tablespoons of flour, mix, and allow to cook a minute. Pour in a cup of milk gradually and cook, stirring constantly, until the sauce is thick and creamy. Then add 2 tablespoons of Parmesan cheese, 2 tablespoons of Worcestershire or A-1 Sauce, a dash of salt, and some ground black pepper.

Now *crumble* a half pound of hamburger into a skillet with a little butter, push it around until it is browned, and add to the sauce. Next add the beaten yolks of five eggs. Cook all this for just a moment, then take it off the fire and beat it well. Cool it.

Beat the egg whites until they are creamy. When the yolk mixture is cool, take a big spoonful of the whites and fold it in very thoroughly, until you have a slightly foamy look. Then pour the mixture slowly over the remaining egg whites, and gently fold and cut and lift as you pour. Now slide all this into a buttered and floured soufflé dish and bake in a 350° oven for a good twenty-five minutes, or maybe a little more. This soufflé should be firm; when you test it, it should shake hardly at all.

This makes a fine lunch. With a plate of hot buttered toast, and a dish of cold pickled beets—you want something spicy—you will have a good meal.

CHICKEN AND ALMOND SOUFFLÉ

Something fine.

In the top of a double boiler melt 3 tablespoons of butter, stir in 3 tablespoons of flour, cook a minute, then add one half cup each of heavy cream and chicken broth. Stir constantly until the mixture is thick and smooth.

Now add a cup and a half of finely minced chicken. *Finely* minced. (Egg whites are strong but they are not strong enough to lift a chicken leg.)

Next, a half cup of almond meal. (And where do you get almond meal? Well, you can buy blanched almonds in a can. Take about eight ounces—that's a can—and put the almonds in a blender. Hold your hand on the lid of the blender before you flip the switch, otherwise they'll knock the lid off. By the time the almonds stop jumping around, you'll have almond meal. If you haven't a blender, you might try a meat grinder, or just go after them with a hammer.)

Add some pepper, but be careful with salt. There is probably some in the chicken broth. Taste the sauce and see what you think.

Add now five beaten egg yolks, stir and cook for just a minute. Take off the fire, add a tablespoon of sherry, beat, and let cool.

Beat six egg whites stiff. Take a large spoonful of them

and fold determinedly into the chicken mixture until it looks slightly foamy. Now pour the mixture over the remaining egg whites and fold and cut gently and thoroughly.

Then slip it into a buttered and floured soufflé dish and bake in a 350° oven for twenty-five minutes. Test it.

Start this meal off with melon and ham. You know how to do that: slice a sweet honeydew into thin wedges and then peel each wedge. Buy thin slices of *prosciutto* or Westphalian ham (the Westphalian has more taste) and cover each wedge of melon with ham. Let each eater grind as much black pepper over the ham as he likes.

Next the soufflé with a platter of fresh string beans which you have French-cut and slightly undercooked.

Then a salad of Belgian endive with French dressing. You need something bitter.

And that's all.

CORN SOUFFLÉ

Possibly the easiest of them all is this corn soufflé. You need merely a can of *cream*-style corn and four eggs.

Separate the eggs. Beat the yolks well, dump the can of corn into them and mix. Add a dash of cayenne pepper.

Beat the whites as you have been told, spoon a quarter of them into the corn, and mix thoroughly, thoroughly. Then gently pour the corn over the remaining egg whites and fold carefully until you have a good light mass.

17

+ floured?

See p. 10

Put all this into a buttered soufflé dish and into a 350° oven. Twenty minutes should do it, but test to be sure. It may need a couple of minutes more.

This is really a fine, safe, amateur soufflé. You have to be marvellously inept for it to fail. While it is not a dish that will bowl over the chef of the Ritz in Paris, say, it has a pleasant flavor and should give you confidence.

You have some cold lamb. Slice it very thin, make a sauce to go with it by beating together half French mustard and half mayonnaise. With a salad and the soufflé, you have a meal that appears to have been given some thought. Yet, really, what is it? Left-over lamb and a can of corn.

SPINACH SOUFFLÉ

A surprisingly good dish, and simple enough.

Buy a package of frozen *chopped* spinach, and cook it as you are instructed on the box.

When you are finished, you will find you have rather damp spinach. This must be corrected, for water is the enemy of the soufflé. So, squeeze and pour off what liquid you can, then put the spinach in a pan with a little butter over good heat and shake it until all the moisture seems driven off. Don't burn it, naturally.

(Of course you *should* do all this with fresh spinach—two pounds—wash, boil, chop, dry, but *will* you?)

Now in a double boiler make the sauce of 3 tablespoons of butter, 3 tablespoons of flour, and a cup of liquid that is half chicken broth and half milk. Stir this constantly

18

till it is good and thick. Add pepper and salt and a big squeeze of lemon juice, then dump in the spinach and beat till everything is well combined. Then remove from the heat and cool.

Separate five eggs. Beat the yolks into the spinach mixture, then beat the whites till properly stiff. Take a big spoonful of the whites and stir it into the spinach until the mixture looks foamy. Then gently dribble the mixture over the rest of the egg whites and fold, fold, fold. Pour into a buttered and floured soufflé dish and bake in a 350° oven for twenty-five minutes. Test it.

Excellent with slices of Virginia ham, but best of all with broiled scallops. See page 118.

Incidentally, if you would like a spinach soufflé to stand alone, for lunch say, add a cup of *finely* chopped ham to the mixture.

TOMATO SOUFFLÉ

It would be nice if you could make a tomato soufflé without trouble. I thought so. I opened a can of tomato soup, added a couple of tablespoons of tomato paste, beat in four egg yolks, then folded in the whites. I baked it in a 350° oven for twenty-five minutes. There is no reason in the world why this shouldn't work. The only trouble is, it doesn't.

Tomatoes do not take kindly to the whole idea of soufflés. They can be forced into it, but always reluctantly.

19

This will work:

Chop up six medium-sized tomatoes. Put a little butter in a pan and cook them over lowish heat. As they soften, stir and mash them. The idea is to drive the water off, and they will be done—this may take twenty minutes— when they "blop" instead of boil. Now push them through a sieve to get rid of the skins and seeds.

In the top of a double boiler melt 3 tablespoons of butter, add 3 tablespoons of flour, cook, add a cup of milk, and stir till you have a good thick sauce. Add the tomato purée, 2 tablespoons of tomato paste, and then 2 tablespoons of Parmesan cheese. Cook all this for a couple of minutes and beat smooth.

Take the top of the double boiler off its water and cool the mixture a bit. Then add the beaten yolks of five eggs. Cool it more.

Beat five egg whites. Take a big spoonful of them and combine thoroughly with the tomato mixture, until you get the foamy look. Then gently pour this sauce over the remaining egg whites and fold gently, gently. Now slip it all into a buttered and floured soufflé dish and bake twenty-five minutes in a 350° oven.

At the end, test it, of course.

After all this effort you will have a tomato soufflé, not one of the great high trembling beauties—in fact, it probably won't do more than rise to the top of the dish—but it will taste extremely good and give you a certain feeling of triumph.

Eat with it, veal—scallops fried lightly in butter and served with anchovy butter.

20

Have you the patience and ability to make a chicken Jeanette? In the summer it makes a fine display with a tomato soufflé. Or, failing that, try cold corned beef with fresh horseradish.

CORNMEAL SOUFFLÉ

In a saucepan heat two cups of milk almost to a boil.

Be careful with this, keep the flame always low. Add now one third of a cup of cornmeal, 1 tablespoon of butter, and salt and pepper. Cook this and keep stirring until you have achieved a thin gruel.

Take the pot off the fire, add the yolks of four eggs, stir them in thoroughly, and let the mixture cool.

When it is cool, beat five egg whites stiff, then beat a third of them vigorously into the cornmeal mixture. Then dribble the mixture over the remaining whites and fold them in carefully. Slip into a soufflé dish and place in a 350° oven.

About twenty minutes, but test it.

ANCHOVY SOUFFLÉ

In the top of a double boiler melt 3 tablespoons of butter, add 3 tablespoons of flour, mix, cook for a minute, and then pour in a cup of chicken broth. Cook this, stirring, until you have a thick white sauce.

Open a two-ounce can of anchovies (the rolled fillets

with capers and olive oil), put a little more than half of them into a bowl and mash them to a paste with a wooden spoon.

Add them to the white sauce, mix thoroughly, take the top of the double boiler off the hot water, stir in four egg yolks, and let the mixture cool.

Beat five egg whites stiff and proceed to combine the soufflé as usual.

This should take about twenty minutes in a 350° oven. But test it.

CLAM SOUFFLÉ

This, like a corn soufflé, is extremely simple to make.

Buy two seven-ounce cans of minced clams. Drain all the juice away. Put the clams now in a bowl, add a dash of cayenne and the yolks of five eggs, mix thoroughly.

Beat six egg whites stiff and combine with the clams in the usual way.

This makes a fine first course and perhaps you would like to serve it in individual soufflé dishes. If so, divide the batter into no more than four parts, bake the individual dishes in a 350° oven for twelve to fifteen minutes. If you are using one large dish, it will take twenty to twenty-two minutes.

LOBSTER SOUFFLÉ

The sensible way to make this is to buy a pound of already cooked fresh lobster meat.

In the top of a double boiler combine 3 tablespoons of butter with 3 tablespoons of flour, add a good half cup of milk and a good half cup of chicken broth.

Stir until you have a white sauce, and add a cup of freshly grated Parmesan cheese and a dash of cayenne. Keep stirring until you have a smooth mixture. Take the pot off the fire, and mix 2 tablespoons of sauce with the lobster meat which you have cut up. Now put this lobster in the bottom of a soufflé dish.

To the remainder of the cheese sauce add five egg yolks and stir thoroughly.

Beat six egg whites stiff, combine them in the usual way with the cheese mixture, and pour over the lobster.

This will take twenty or twenty-five minutes in a 350° oven.

DESSERT SOUFFLÉS
✳

VANILLA SOUFFLÉ

Bland, but classic.

Melt 2 tablespoons of butter in the top of double boiler. Mix in 2 tablespoons of flour. Cook a minute, add a cup of hot milk, one half cup of sugar, and, if you have it, a one-inch piece of vanilla bean. If no vanilla bean, a quarter of a teaspoon of vanilla extract, but *after* the mixture has cooked.

Stir this constantly until it's thick and smooth. Remove from the fire, and discard the vanilla bean. (*Now* add the vanilla extract if that's what you're doing.)

Beat five egg yolks and add to the sauce. Let it cool.

Beat six egg whites till they are stiff, then add a large spoonful of them to the vanilla mixture, and fold it in thoroughly until the mixture has a slightly foamy texture.

Now, dribble all over the remaining egg whites and fold carefully, carefully, until all is mixed thoroughly. Slide this into a buttered and sugared soufflé dish and

24

place in a 350° oven. Twenty minutes, or maybe a little longer should do for this.

Test it.

Crushed fruit—strawberries, raspberries, or blueberries with some sugar and Kirsch on them—is probably as pleasant a sauce as you can find for this soufflé. Or, if you have a good recipe for a cold lemon sauce you might try it. But whatever you use, have it cold.

To precede this soufflé, try to get a couple of fresh Cornish hens. Stuff them with cooked, wild rice, mushrooms, and chopped walnuts, and while they are roasting baste them with currant jelly. Some thinly sliced fresh carrots cooked in sparkling soda (a split of White Rock) are good with this, and so is a water-cress salad.

In the summertime try this:

Cut off the stems of a couple of bunches of water cress. Chop leaves coarsely; mix them with a cup of mayonnaise and spread in the bottom of a large oblong glass baking dish. Set aside.

In a large shallow baking pan, buttered, place four fillets of sole, topped with more butter and lemon juice, and bake in a moderate oven for about twenty minutes, until done. Remove from oven and let cool.

When the fish are cool, carefully, with a spatula, arrange them on top of the water cress. Pour two cans of consommé (the kind that jells) over all this, and set it in the icebox for three or four hours. Unless you are awfully hungry, this, with some hot rolls and the soufflé, should be dinner.

CHOCOLATE SOUFFLÉ

Here is the greatest of the dessert soufflés.

In the top of a double boiler melt 3 tablespoons of butter and mix in 3 tablespoons of flour. Cook a moment. Then add a cup of hot milk, and stir constantly until the mixture is rich and creamy.

Add one half cup of sugar. Stir until dissolved. Add three squares (three ounces) of bitter cooking chocolate broken in two, at least. This will take a moment to dissolve.

The mixture will appear grainy for a while but, as you keep stirring, suddenly the chocolate will combine and you will have a smooth, thick, elegant sauce.

Take this off the fire. Add a dash of salt and beat the mixture for a minute. Allow it to cool a bit, then add five beaten egg yolks to it, and beat until smooth.

Beat seven egg whites until stiff. When the sauce is really cool, take a large spoonful of them and fold vigorously into the chocolate mixture until it appears slightly foamy. Then dribble this sauce over the remaining egg whites and fold thoroughly and carefully.

Slide all this into a buttered and sugared soufflé dish and place in a 350° oven. At the end of twenty minutes, if the gods are good, you should have something wonderful. But test it.

Here's a fine, simple, perfect sauce: Beat a half pint of

heavy cream until it's stiff. Allow a half pint of vanilla ice cream to soften—not melt, soften. Then beat these two together. Add a couple of tablespoons of good brandy.

Have yourself a fine dinner with this. Have a roast rolled fillet of beef; have fresh asparagus; have potatoes Anna. And for a salad, Belgian endive with slices of *foie gras* on it and French dressing.

COFFEE SOUFFLÉ

Melt 2 tablespoons of butter in the top of a double boiler and mix in 2 tablespoons of flour. Cook a minute. Add a half cup of hot milk and a half cup of strong, strong black coffee. (Make this coffee as you will, but if you use instant, be sure that it is triple strength.) Add one half cup of sugar and cook and stir constantly until the mixture is well combined. Set off the fire.

Beat four egg yolks and when the mixture is slightly cool, add them to it.

Beat five egg whites until stiff. When the mixture is really cool, add a large spoonful of the whites and combine thoroughly with it, then add this to the remaining egg whites, and fold and fold and fold, gently.

Pour this into a buttered and sugared soufflé dish and put into a 350° oven. This should take twenty or twenty-two minutes. Test it.

The best sauce for this coffee soufflé is simply whipped cream, thoroughly chilled. If you want to add a little brandy, go ahead.

You might well have a steak before this, and some broiled tomatoes, and some very small baked potatoes. This should make you feel well on a dreary winter evening.

Or on a summer evening you might try slices of cold roast beef and a horseradish mousse:

HORSERADISH MOUSSE

Dissolve two envelopes of unflavored gelatin in a half cup of chicken broth, then melt it in another cup and a half of hot chicken broth. Set this aside to cool. Grate three quarters of a cup of fresh horseradish; grate the rind of a lemon; grate a medium-sized onion. Combine these and season with a scant teaspoon of salt.

Beat three egg whites stiff.

Pour the cooled chicken broth, it must be very cool, into the horseradish mixture, and then fold in the egg whites. Now pour all this into a mold you have first rinsed in very cold water, then place in the icebox until the mousse is firm.

LEMON SOUFFLÉ

This, for some reason, is extraordinarily better than you would think.

In the top of the double boiler melt 2 tablespoons of

butter, mix in 2 tablespoons flour. Cook a minute. Then add a cup of heavy cream. Stir this—and it won't take long—until it is rich and smooth. Take off the heat to cool.

Beat four egg yolks with a scant half cup of sugar. Add to the sauce and beat all together.

Take a large, fresh lemon and grate finely all of its rind into a bowl. Add the juice from that lemon and one other.

Beat five egg whites till they are stiff and glistening. When the egg-cream mixture is cool, add the lemon juice and rind, beat well.

Take a large spoonful of the whites and mix well into the lemon sauce until it appears slightly foamy. Dribble the sauce over the remaining egg whites and lift and fold gently and thoroughly.

Finally, slide all into a buttered and sugared soufflé dish and then into a 350° oven for twenty to twenty-five minutes. Test it.

For a sauce, try this. Cut up a couple of cups of fresh strawberries—large ones in quarters, small ones in halves. Melt 2 or 3 tablespoons of red currant jelly and pour over the berries with a sprinkle of Kirsch, if you will. Put this in the icebox for a couple of hours to get cold, cold, cold.

The temperature is important. A certain amount of the pleasure of this dessert is the contrast of cold strawberries and hot lemon.

Why not have for this dinner a lemon sole? And some of those whole, baby Belgian carrots, and a large cucumber salad.

Or it's not bad after a leg of lamb and little potatoes and

a big platter of fresh asparagus. I don't suppose you could make a hollandaise sauce, so put lots of butter on the asparagus.

(By the way, you can make an excellent orange soufflé by substituting for the lemon rind and juice the finely grated rind of one good-sized orange and the juice of that orange. You might add a tablespoon of Cointreau if you please. The same strawberry sauce is excellent with this.)

STRAWBERRY SOUFFLÉ

In the top of a double boiler melt 2 tablespoons of butter. Mix in 2 tablespoons of flour. To this add one cup of hot milk. Stir constantly until rich and smooth. Set off the fire.

In a saucepan, mix one cup of crushed strawberries with half a cup of sugar. Boil this for a while—anyway five minutes—until it seems well combined. Mix this into the white sauce.

Beat five egg yolks, and when the sauce has cooled a bit, add them to it. This is a good time to add a tablespoon of brandy, if you want it.

Beat six egg whites until stiff; then, when the sauce is really cool, take a generous spoonful of the whites and mix them thoroughly, thoroughly into the sauce. Now pour the sauce over the remainder of the egg whites and fold—thoroughly, lightly.

Slide into a buttered and sugared soufflé dish and place in a 350° oven. This should take about twenty to twenty-five minutes. Serve with sliced strawberries which have a little melted red currant jelly poured over them.

This is fine in summer when strawberries have a real taste.

You could have it after lemon chicken (page 119), fresh buttered green peas, and sliced beefsteak tomatoes which have been dribbled with olive oil and vinegar and sprinkled with fresh sweet basil and freshly ground black pepper.

If you use frozen strawberries for the soufflé, be sure their juice is boiled long enough with the sugar to make a syrup.

PEACH SOUFFLÉ

Purée enough fresh, sweet peaches to make a cupful. Put this in a saucepan, squeeze the juice of half a lemon over it, and add a half cup of sugar. Boil this for two or three minutes, or until the sugar is completely dissolved. Set aside and cool.

Beat until stiff seven or eight egg whites.* When the peaches are cool, take a big spoonful of the whites and fold it into them to lighten the mixture. Then pour these peaches over the remaining egg whites and fold all carefully.

* Seven or eight egg whites. This is something you might not normally have lying around the kitchen. And it seems a shame to throw that many egg yolks away.

You can acquire them by accumulation if, during the week, you have need of yolks for something—maybe you have the good fortune to know how to make a *crème brûlée*. If not, see page 163.

Now slide this into a buttered and sugared soufflé dish and place in a 350° oven. Watch this soufflé. It should be ready in eighteen or twenty minutes. Test it.

At its best this is a seasonal dish. You should make it during the time the peaches are at their largest and sweetest and best, because with it you should serve a large bowl of freshly sliced raw peaches made cold, cold, cold in the icebox.

The soufflé is really nothing more than a flavored puff, and for its best enjoyment you need the contrast in texture and temperature of the cold, fresh peaches.

In the winter it can, of course, be made with those sliced, frozen things.

Try this some time when you are having cold, sliced Virginia ham, say, and artichokes. (Artichokes taste better if you boil them with an onion, sliced, a whole lemon, quartered, salt, a few pepper corns, and a tablespoon of olive oil.)

GRAND MARNIER SOUFFLÉ

Maybe some midnight you would like a simple Grand Marnier soufflé with nothing before it and nothing after it. Here's what you do:

In the top of a double boiler mix 3 tablespoons of butter with 2 of flour. Cook this a moment and then add a cup of heavy cream. Stir this until it thickens.

Add now 6 tablespoons of sugar, and when the sugar has dissolved remove the pan from the fire and stir in five egg yolks. Stir in also 5 tablespoons of Grand Marnier. Let the mixture cool.

When it is cool, beat the whites of six eggs stiff and combine the soufflé as you have been told.

Finally, slip the mixture into a buttered and sugared soufflé dish and cook for about twenty minutes in a 350° oven.

If you want to do something fancy you can soak halves of small lady fingers in Grand Marnier and lay them in the middle of the soufflé—that is, pour half the mixture into the soufflé dish, arrange the lady fingers on that, and then top with the remaining mixture.

So, good luck and good appetite. I hope that noise I hear isn't the thud of soufflés falling all over the nation.

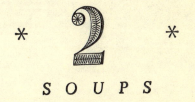

* **2** *

SOUPS

*

Here is about as simple a recipe for a dish of soup as you could find: Take a quart of water, add half a dozen cloves of garlic, salt and pepper, boil all together for ten minutes, and then pour over toast. It is French of course; it is economical, it is easy, it is even homeopathic, for its addicts say it is good for cramps.

But whatever its virtues, it has its drawbacks—taste, I should think, not least among them. It recommends itself to me as a dish you serve to someone you know very well and don't particularly like. Of course, you can try to snob it up. You can say, "This is the famous *aigo-bouido, just* as it is made in the Basses-Alpes," but say what you will, you are going to be stuck with boiled water.

But let us suppose you invite to your house only people you like, and who are not the victims of cramps. There are a number of pleasant ways to make soup—out of anything really, from sardines to strawberries.

The making of the great consommés from scratch—beginning with water and beef or veal or chicken or fish—is a long, tedious, and rewarding process. Let us suppose you know how to make them—any decent cookbook will tell you—or let us rather suppose, regrettably, that what you do is open a can of the stuff. Whatever your method, use the best you can find, for on the strength, flavor, and clarity of consommé depends much of the goodness of most soups.

With plain consommé there isn't much you can do except drink it in good health. A thousand things are possible—adding rice or tapioca or one of the innumerable *pastas,* or croutons or juliennes of carrots or beans or leeks or whatever—but they don't really add much to the enjoyment of a good consommé. About the only thing I could recommend is slices of ripe avocado. Somehow this makes a diversion.

I go to a house where no matter what the first course—a cold artichoke vinaigrette, crêpes stuffed with crab, a slice of pâté—you are always served a cup of hot consommé at the same time. This is when it is best, in contrast. It also clears your mouth for what is to come.

COLD SOUPS
*

GAZPACHOS

Here are some gazpacho variations. They must always be served ice cold, even the plates *must* be chilled.

Peel, seed, and chop fine two tomatoes, a cucumber, a sweet red pepper. Chop a fair-sized sweet onion fine as well.

Put all these in a big bowl and add four tablespoons of olive oil. Then pour over them four cups of cold veal broth.

And where will you get veal broth? This way: in two quarts of water put a half pound of raw cubed veal and a half head of lettuce, chopped, and salt and pepper. Boil this until the liquid is reduced by about half, or upon tasting you have something rich and fine. *Don't* pour it over the vegetables until it is cold. In fact, make it long before. Serves 6.

Another one: Peel, seed, and chop fine two tomatoes, a cucumber, a sweet pepper, and chop fine an onion. Mix these in a bowl with three or four heaping tablespoons of sour cream—enough to coat them well. When you are ready to serve this, pour over it four or five cups of icy chicken broth. Salt and ground pepper at the table. Serves 6.

A third: Chop fine a half pound of cooked shrimps. Peel, seed, and chop fine a cucumber. Grate a good-sized onion. Seed and chop fine half a sweet red pepper. Mix these in a bowl and chill them.

Now, add two and a half cups of chicken broth to two and a half cups of buttermilk. Chill. Pour over the vegetables and shrimps. Serves 6-8.

And don't be frightened about the buttermilk. Even people who loathe buttermilk gulp this down without a murmur.

FRUIT SOUPS

You don't run into fruit soups very often, and for a proper reason: They are not very good. Soups, generally, should urge you on to the rest of the meal, but most fruit soups, sweet, spiced, and loaded with wine, don't promise or suggest anything.

However, there are exceptions.

A cherry soup: Stem and seed enough big black sweet cherries to make two cups. Put them in a pan with just enough water to cover and let them simmer for ten or twelve minutes. Now add a tablespoon of honey and the juice of a lemon. Stir this up and pour it into a bowl, and add four cups of cold borsch. (The bottled kind will do, but strain out the beets.)

This must be served very cold. It isn't bad on a summer night if you are going to have cold baked ham after it. If you like sour cream, add a blop to each serving. Serves 6.

An apple soup: Peel, core, and chop up enough tart apples to make four cups. Put them in a pan and add a dash of salt, the grated rind of a lemon, a scant tablespoon of cinnamon, and a half cup of sugar. Just cover with water and simmer until the apples are soft. Then purée the apples either in a blender or through a sieve.

Now add the juice of that lemon, a tablespoon of melted currant jelly, and three cups of red wine—good wine, and dry. Chill this well. Serves 4-6.

Not bad to have before something heavy, like sauerbraten and dumplings.

FROM THE SEA
✳

In Venice, in the winter, you go to Harry's Bar. You have lunch there, you have dinner there; you have lunch there, you have dinner there. And if you are sensible, you often have his fish soup.

41

Frankly, I am too timid to ask a restaurant proprietor how to make a dish, but Natalie Schafer is not. She asked Harry and she got the recipe. Here it is:

3 *pounds of salt-water fish (bass, snapper or such—or a combination)*
2 *tomatoes*
2 *medium onions*
5 *stalks of celery*
1 *parsley root*
a pinch of saffron

Peel the tomatoes and onions and chop them and the other vegetables fine. Put them, with the fish and the saffron, in a big pot and cover with water. Cook until the fish is done, about 20 minutes.

When it is, take it out and remove the skin and *all* the bones. Test the vegetables; when they are soft, press them, and the fish, through a sieve. Or better still, if you have a blender, run everything in it until smooth. Add just enough salt and ground pepper to taste.

Just before serving, when you are reheating, swirl in a few drops of olive oil.

Of course this makes quite a lot of soup. But it freezes successfully. (About six good bowlfuls.)

OYSTER STEW

Buy a half dozen oysters for each person. Have the fish man open them and *save the liquor.*

Into a pan put the juice, a lump of butter, a dash of

celery salt, paprika, a dash of Worcestershire sauce. Add enough half-and-half—milk and cream—to provide a good bowlful for each portion. Heat this and then add the oysters. Simmer just long enough for the oysters to plump up a bit. Then add another lump of soft butter, more paprika, and serve.

Very good. Not served nearly often enough.

CLAM STEW

Almost the same as for oysters. Buy small clams—little necks—put the liquor and butter in a pan, but *no* Worcestershire this time. Better a grind of black pepper than paprika, also. And no salt.

Add the half-and-half, and get this hot but not boiling before you put in the clams.

Now, when you add the clams, cook for only one minute, or less. Just long enough to heat the clams. Cooking toughens clams.

Add a final swirl of butter, and serve.

There are some *whole* canned clams that you can use satisfactorily if you can't get fresh.

BILLI-BI

A rare and excellent soup. It was created, a good many years ago, at Maxim's in Paris, for William B. Leeds, a tin-plate tycoon—hence the name.

43

Buy eighteen mussels. Scrub them clean in cold water.

In a pot put 4 tablespoons of chopped onions and 3 tablespoons of chopped shallots.

Add three cups of heavy cream, two cups of *good* dry white wine, and the mussels.

Add a dash of salt and pepper, and a trace of cayenne.

Heat this all till it boils up in a foam, then reduce the flame and cook ten minutes. Finally, pour through a sieve lined with cheese cloth.

That's it. A fine, high-toned soup. Only the fanciest eaters will know what they're getting.

If you want it cold, be sure it is *very* cold, and serve with a grind of black pepper. Serves 5-6.

By the way, *never* put the mussels back in the soup. But eat them, by all means. The cook's bonus.

FROM ITALY
✳

Minestrone is a variable soup; it does not turn out the same twice. This is by design.

Here is a breathless recipe Ruth Norman had from Burr Tillstrom—that same Burr Tillstrom who has achieved a certain fame as the friend of Kukla, Beulah Witch, and Oliver J. Dragon:

"Marcello Franchini, my good friend from Rome, had

been hungering for some *real* minestrone for a long time. I had better explain that his wife, Barbara—she's from Rockford, Illinois—met him on a train from Paris to Rome when she was working in the American Embassy in France and that she had never learned to cook even American style, so after marriage and settling down in Chicago she attempted to translate some of his mother's famous Roman recipes. The words came out fine—she's a whiz at languages—but how do you figure a direction like '. . . a spoonful of such and such' when you don't know which spoon, or '. . . two fingers of,' or '. . . a glass of,' or 'cook until done,' etc. etc. . . . all excellent clues for people who know how to cook 'by ear,' as my mother says, but no good for Barbara.

"So, having a taster's knowledge of minestrone, and access to a couple of good cookbooks, I suggested that we pool our efforts. After all, my Swedish-Yankee families made great soups, Barbara was a good translator, and Marcello's taste buds had a strong memory. It was decided that the minestrone should be started at my house. Barbara and Marcello were living in a small apartment behind their shop—did I say they have a wonderful Italian boutique here in Chicago?—and we thought the glorious odors of cooking soup might interfere with business, especially since I insisted on the purist touch, starting from scratch and making the stock.

"Early in the morning of the now famous day I began the operation in the kitchen of my coach-house studio. I bought a couple of huge beef bones, three veal joints, and three pounds of soup meat.

"In a large pot—I used an oval cast-iron French one—
I browned the meat and the bones, which had been ever
so lightly floured, in a little olive oil. Then I added water
to cover everything completely. Then into the pot went
leeks, parsley, and celery, all tied in a bundle, also three
medium chopped onions and a couple of cloves of
chopped garlic. And fresh-ground pepper, salt, basil, and
marjoram.

"We all agreed that minestrone had beans, so I set
some good old navy beans to soak for about three hours—
maybe a little longer.

"Of course I skimmed the scum whenever it accumu-
lated, and after five hours of cooking I added the beans—
with the water they had soaked in—and simmered everything for another two hours. When I added the beans I
fished out the bundle of leeks and celery and parsley.

"At this point I turned off the stove and called a cab.
It was dinnertime. I rushed into the shop, grazing a last
customer with my still red-hot pot of soup. Italian and
English flooded the Franchinis' kitchen, lips smacked and
nostrils flared, eyes glowed, especially those of Marcello's
two blond children.

"Someone said potatoes, someone said rice, everyone
agreed on pasta, and green beans, carrots, peas, more
chopped onions, more parsley, more celery—so all of
these went into the pot which was again steaming and
simmering.

"About proportions: There were three medium potatoes, cubed; three quarters of a pound of green beans, cut

in half-inch lengths; two stalks of cut up celery; two small onions, diced; a small handful of cut parsley. We let these cook for about twenty-five minutes, then we added a handful of rice, a half pound of fresh peas, and five medium carrots, sliced.

"Then, when the peas and carrots were almost done, we threw in a handful of *rigatoni,* which is large *pasta,* and then, for a finishing touch, two or three heaping tablespoons of freshly grated Parmesan cheese. There was a bit more salt and pepper to taste.

"Then with salad, a good Italian bread, more Parmesan, a little wine, some fruit and *espresso,* it was a glorious success—a full meal, which Marcello said was often the case in his family—just as a thick vegetable soup is a whole meal in our house, particularly on a cold wintery day.

"There are many other things that can be used too. Zucchini, for example, and tomatoes. I personally don't care for tomatoes in soup, so I voted them out. Spinach is another suggestion, and fresh basil is wonderful. In Italy they use whatever vegetables are in season—but in this country we have so much available all the time that with us it is a matter of choice, actually.

"Of course, if the soup is too thick, add a little more water, but you want it thick, almost like a loose stew. The meat is miraculous after all that cooking, tender and full of flavor."

There you have minestrone. And a day's work cut out

for you. If there are any faint hearts present, let them be advised you can buy minestrone in cans. But oh, the difference.

Here are a couple of other Italian soups that are worth mentioning.

PAVESE

For each person you need an egg, a large cup of consommé, two slices of Italian bread, Parmesan.

Sprinkle Parmesan on the bread, shove it into a hot oven to toast. In the boiling consommé, poach the egg lightly. In a large soup plate center the egg, flank it with the toast and pour the hot consommé over all. Sprinkle with Parmesan.

If you are ever sick in Italy—and you may well be— this soup is a godsend. Any restaurant will make it for you.

CHICKEN CUSTARD IN BROTH

This soup was told me by an ancient countess who had heavy eyelids, fingers covered with dirty diamonds, and a forty-five-inch waistline. But she knew how to eat.

I have simplified it a bit, but the results are the same. In a blender put a half pound of cooked chopped chicken meat, a third of a cup of chicken broth, four eggs, about half a cup of grated Parmesan, salt and pepper. Blend this thoroughly until it is completely smooth, then spoon it into six little buttered ramekins. Set the ramekins in a pan of hot water, and cook over not very high heat until the custard is set—twelve or fifteen minutes should do it.

Now unmold each ramekin into a soup plate, and surround the custard with hot chicken broth.

This is extremely good and something you don't run into every day.

LEFTOVERS
✳

SOMETHING HEAVY:
PEAS PORRIDGE

When you have had a baked ham, and you've eaten it and eaten it until you can't face the sight of it any longer, do this:

Buy a pound of split peas. Get out your biggest pot, toss them into it, throw in the ham bone, three good-sized onions, peeled and chopped, a good dash of tarragon, a handful of minced parsley, and an overgenerous grinding of fresh black pepper. Fill the pot with about three quarts of water, so that it more than covers everything.

Bring to a boil, skim off the scum, then reduce the heat till the pot merely burbles, and let it go. Stir occasionally and cook uncovered. This will take a long time, five or six hours, and is done when everything has melted to a thick purée—except the ham bone, of course.

Now fish out the bone, put it on a platter and let it cool. Also fish out whatever hunks of ham fat you can find and throw them away. When the bone is cool, cut off any meat remaining on it and return this to the pot.

This is an extraordinarily rich soup and cheap, too, since by the time you make it you have forgotten you paid for the ham.

There will be a lot left over. Pour it into little loaf pans and chill it in the icebox. It will solidify and you can use it, sliced, the next night with cocktails, spread on toast or crackers. Not bad, and you can say you made it yourself. Serves 6-8.

MORE WITH LEFTOVER
HAM

At Christmastime people *will* send you smoked Virginia hams. Well: Cover the bottom of a big soup pot with slices of the ham. Chop some parsley fine, sprinkle it over the ham, grind black pepper on it. Cut a fresh young cabbage in quarters, lay over the parsley.

Mix a couple of cans of consommé with a couple of cans of chicken broth. Pour enough of this into the pot to cover the cabbage. Now simmer. You will have to keep adding more broth, because the cabbage will eat it up. The soup will be done when a fork runs easily into the cabbage. You can't say exactly because cabbage varies. But don't let it get mushy.

Serve the ham and cabbage in big soup plates. Strain the broth and pour over. Hearty.

LEFTOVER SALAD SOUP

The day will surely come when you have, in your exuberance, made a tremendous mixed green salad, covered it with a proper oil and vinegar dressing, and then find that nobody wants much of it.

Well, courage.

Leave your guests, hurry to your blender, pour into it two cups of consommé or chicken broth, and add a tablespoon of flour. Run the blender till the flour is absorbed. Then begin piling in the salad—be sure all the dressing gets in—until you have a very thick purée.

This has to be cooked. Preferably in a double boiler and for at least an hour. Stir it occasionally.

This makes a remarkably good potage, with a surprising bite from the vinegar.

These proportions suppose a great deal of leftover salad. Be sensible. If you haven't much salad, use less consommé and flour. What you wish to produce is a thick soup.

CREAM SOUPS
✳

These are not the classic creams of high French cooking, but they will do, they will do. As always, their excellence depends on the freshness of their components—and their speed of making, on the indispensable blender.

CARROT

Slice enough carrots to make two cupfuls. Cook them until they are just tender. Drain and dump into a blender. Add a cup and a half of well-seasoned chicken broth. Run blender at full speed until the soup is very smooth, then add a half pint of light cream. Let go another thirty seconds. Serves 4-6.

Heat this soup in a double boiler.

(You can substitute, with great success, a can of baby Belgian whole carrots for the fresh.)

CHICKEN

You have a couple of cups of—probably leftover—cooked chicken meat. Mince it and put it into a blender with a cup and a half of chicken broth and a half pint of light cream. Run at full speed till you have a smooth liquid. Again, heat in a double boiler. Serves 4-6.

You get the idea. A number of other soups can be made in exactly the same way. Let me make clear that their final taste will depend on the potency and seasoning of the chicken broth. Perhaps you had better make that yourself to be sure?

Anyway, for the carrots you can substitute two cups of cooked cauliflower fleurettes; or a couple of cups of cooked corn, cut off the cob; or cooked fresh celery; or barely cooked spinach; or if you have a garden and will promise to use the peas within an hour of picking them, try it with a cup and a half of *raw* peas; or artichoke bottoms—you can buy these in jars; or the tips of cooked fresh asparagus; or diced fresh mushrooms, which have first been cooked for fifteen minutes in a little butter (use juice and all); or cooked fresh shrimps (some curry powder added); or cooked fresh squash, although this is pretty bland; or boiled onions; or; or; what do you like?

Of course taste these soups before you serve them, they may need a little something: more salt or pepper, or if they are too thick, a touch more broth or cream.

TOMATO

This is a little more trouble.

Peel four medium tomatoes, take out the seeds. Mince half a good-sized onion. Chop up a quarter of a green pepper. Slice a stalk of celery. Mince about a tablespoon of parsley.

Put these all in a pan with a tablespoon of butter and cook them slowly until they melt—about fifteen or twenty minutes. Keep stirring them, so they don't stick.

When they are done, cool them, then throw them all into the blender, add a cup and a half of chicken broth and a half pint of light cream. Run the blender till the soup is smooth.

This *must* be heated in a double boiler, and carefully. It must not boil, for if it does something unexpected and unpleasant will happen.

Taste for seasoning. You will likely want more salt and pepper.

You can save yourself a certain amount of trouble if you will buy a can of *stewed* tomatoes, the kind that already has celery and onion and such in it. Put the whole can in the blender, add not quite so much chicken broth —there's juice in the can—and the cream, and proceed as above. Serves 4-6.

Eat well. Soup is a comfort at the beginning of a meal and we all need what comfort we can get.

* 3 *

CRÊPES

*

Consider the crêpe Suzette. A famous dessert—
maybe the most famous—it is a pretty thing to see: the
thinnest of pancakes boiling in an outrageous sauce, wait-
ers hovering, captains concentrating, aromas rising, blue
flames dripping from silver spoons.

And it is not only a spectacle. Listen as Mrs. Rombauer,
that most celebrated and practical of American house-
hold goddesses, clasps her floured hands and lets a sigh es-
cape her kind Midwestern heart. " . . . about as good to
eat," she says, "as anything man or superman can make."

Crêpes Suzette, of course, were devised in France, but as foods go they are not particularly old—sixty or sixty-five years. After their popularity was established a number of chefs naturally claimed to have invented them: The first man said he had thought of them in 1904, but there were soon others who vowed to have made them in 1900, then 1898, then 1897. The best story, however, is that of Henri Charpentier, a famous French cook who spent most of his life in America, who waited till all the furor had died down, and then said, oh no, *he* had created them and in *1894*.

In Monte Carlo, too. Albert, Prince of Wales, Victoria's son, and a celebrated eater, was staying at the hotel where Charpentier worked; the dish was made for him.

And by accident. Charpentier was one evening concocting a complicated sauce to pour over crêpes when suddenly it caught fire. Terrified, because the prince was waiting, he tasted what was in the pan. It was delicious. He plunged the crêpes into it, added more liqueurs, blazed the sauce again, and served it forth.

The prince was delighted, congratulated Charpentier, and then and there the dish was christened Suzette, in honor of a young lady who happened to be dining with the prince.

Well, it has all the elements of a great food story. A glamorous setting, a powerful prince, a beautiful girl, an accident in the kitchen. There is only one drawback to it. In 1894 Henri Charpentier was fourteen years old.

What kind of hotel was the Prince of Wales staying at that had a fourteen-year-old boy doing the cooking?

No matter. Somehow crêpes Suzette came into being. And they have remained rare, gala, and essentially mysterious.

If you take the trouble to examine them, you wonder why. For a crêpe is a pancake, and a pancake may well be, next to roast tiger leg, the oldest cooked food known to man. (You can easily figure it out. On some drowsy paleolithic afternoon, somebody dropped by accident wet meal on a hot stone, and the whole thing began.)

They are made now by everybody all over the world. They are called tortillas or blintzes or popadums or Aunt Minnie's Special Batter Cakes. They have been used for everything from an offering to the gods on Olympus to a hearty breakfast for the truckers on Route 101. (Jupiter was rumored to be especially fond of ones made with honey and cinnamon.)

In England, for hundreds of years—and perhaps still in some sections—pancakes even had a special day, Shrove Tuesday, the day before Lent begins. Lent then was taken with a little more ceremony than it is now, and in preparation for the fast, all the rich things in the house were used up—the eggs, butter, lard, drippings. At eleven o'clock in the morning a bell was rung, called the Pancake Bell, and everyone came to the feast: the apprentices, friends, hangers on, everyone.

There are, conservatively, ten thousand ways to make

pancakes, and they are better or worse depending on the skill of the maker and the appetite of the eater. No one but a fool would presume to say what makes the "best" pancakes, for every cook with a skillet has his own recipe for which he will fight to the death.

It can be said, if timidly, that pancakes, breakfast pancakes, are probably a little more bland than they used to be. One of the great mainstays of the country only a hundred years ago is now almost unheard of and virtually unobtainable: sour-dough pancakes.

For one of the ingredients of sour-dough pancakes is something called a starter. This is a mixture of flour and water and yeast and sugar, which must, however, sit around in a warm place for three days to get itself into shape for use. Not many people will bother with that these days.

The starter does have this virtue: if you take some of it out to make bread or pancakes, you have but to add more flour and water and sugar and it will keep on souring as long as you want.

Our ancestors wanted. Every great-great-grandmother who trundled west in a covered wagon took her jar of starter with her. The reason for this was that she had in those days to use wild yeast: that is, after she mixed flour and water and sugar she had to set her bowl out in the open for five or six days to catch the yeast, which comes with bees or on the wind. This obviously was too awkward a process to go through while traveling. Also, yeast is a plant which is around only in warm weather—in the winter it stays in the ground—so she took her replenishable starter with her. Some of these starters were kept going endlessly, out of pride and convenience. There is one in Oregon that is sixty years old; you can probably find older.

So remember the pioneer spirit as you open your next box of pancake mix: Great-grandmother, in addition to the hazards of the mountains and the plains, the wind and the snow and the rain, in addition to the rude jokes of the wagon drivers and the rude noises of the Indians, great-grandmother had to keep her eye on that goddam jar of starter.

The Forty-Niner was of course called a Sour Dough for the good reason that the dough was the main item of his diet. His starter was something more complicated than the simple flour-yeast-water formula. It contained everything from boiled potatoes to hops; but then, he had further uses for it than pancake-making: The liquid that forms on the top of the mixture as it sours—that is, ferments—can have a considerable effect if drunk.

Make, for old times' sake, a batch of sour-dough pancakes. There is nothing difficult about it—you only need time:

Into a bowl put an envelope or cake of yeast, pour a half cup of luke-warm water over it, stir till it dissolves, then add two more cups of lukewarm water, a tablespoon of salt, a tablespoon of sugar and two cups of sifted flour. Mix up well, cover the bowl. Now keep this in a warm place—78° or 80°—for three days; every morning, give it a good stir. You have your starter.

Now you are ready. Into a bowl measure two cups of the starter. Add a cup of milk, four tablespoons of melted butter, an egg, two tablespoons of sugar, and a dash of salt.

Mix this up. It will probably be too thin. So gradually add flour—you may need up to a cup—until the batter has the consistency of cream.

At the last moment, just before you are ready to cook, dissolve a teaspoon of baking soda in a little water, sprinkle this over the top of the batter, then carefully fold it in.

Now ladle the batter onto a hot griddle or pan and bake as you would any pancake. A stack of these with honey is about as good a breakfast as you can want.

Well, to get back to crêpes, the pancake of the French. As they did with everything else that was handed down to them, the cooks of France examined the wet meal cooked on the hot stone and concluded that improvements were possible. Your paleolithic grandpa wouldn't recognize the old things now.

The crêpe has been developed into an extremely versatile article of food, but, in its variety at least, it is not particularly well known in this country. Which is strange, because in its version as an entrée it is peculiarly adapted to that continuing nightmare of the American cook—leftovers. You can stuff a crêpe with practically anything—ham, chicken, seafood—what have you got?—and come up with a brand-new, excellent dish.

Crêpes, too, have this virtue: Unlike most good things, they *can* be made ahead of time without much loss of quality. Even, if you are hard pressed, they can be frozen. They are best, of course, made and eaten promptly. And, for a wonder, they don't even require courage to cook: just the right size pan and a little good will.

ENTRÉE CRÊPES
✳

Let us save the glory of the Suzette for the end and begin with the crêpe as an entrée.

Here is the basic recipe, which, with variations, does for all crêpes. You need:

> 1 *cup flour*
> ⅛ *teaspoon salt (a good dash)*
> 3 *eggs*
> 7 *teaspoons melted butter*
> 2 *tablespoons brandy or rum*
> 1 *teaspoon grated lemon rind*
> 1½ *cups milk*

Mix all this up gradually—the flour and salt, the eggs and butter, then the seasonings, and finally the milk, until you have a smooth batter the consistency of thin cream, and *no lumps.*

If you're lucky enough to have an electric blender, throw everything into it all at once and run it until the batter is smooth.

63

Now you have to let the batter rest for a couple of hours. Don't ask why. Just do it.

One utensil is necessary for baking crêpes: a small skillet. It should measure approximately six inches across the bottom. There is such a thing as a crêpe pan, which has flaring sides to make it easier to get at the crêpe to turn it, but these pans are hard to come by. An iron skillet will do. Oh, you will also need a spatula.

To cook: Heat the pan and drop into it a small hunk of butter, then tip the pan in all directions so that the bottom surface is well greased. Your heat should be fairly brisk.

Now pour a *small* amount of batter into the pan—not more than 1 to 3 tablespoons, depending on the size of the pan—and *again* tip the pan in all directions *and* immediately, so that this little bit of batter runs over the entire bottom of the pan. This is no trick after you've done it a couple of times.

When you think the cake is cooked—maybe a minute—lift up a corner of it with a spatula and look. If it's a golden brown, it is. Then run the spatula under about a third of the cake and turn it. When *that* side is golden brown, you're done.

Repeat the operation as many times as you need to—always starting with the little hunk of butter. Don't let the skillet get too hot. These cakes burn.

You now have a stack of crêpes keeping warm in the oven. (This recipe should make a dozen and a half

CRÊPES

crêpes.) For an entrée you should have two per person; if you're hungry, more.

One of the great things you can stuff them with is *duxelles*. This is a French concoction that is endlessly useful. To make it, you chop a pound of fresh mushrooms, stems and all, *very fine*. You do the same with a couple of small white onions—or shallots if you can get them.

Then in a big skillet melt a quarter of a pound of butter, add the chopped onions (and a clove of chopped garlic if you like), finally the mushrooms. This must cook very, very slowly. It takes time. All the mushroom juice must be cooked out, the mushrooms must turn black. Then sprinkle with a tablespoon of flour, mix well, and add three tablespoons of cream, salt and pepper, and let all this cook down until it is thickened, blended, and black again.

Now, spoon some of the *duxelles* along the center of one of your hot crêpes, roll each one up and spread a bit more of the *duxelles* on top. In case you are wondering: Don't worry about that word "roll." You can do anything with a crêpe; roll it, fold it in four, even. It will not break.

A couple of these crêpes with a salad and some fruit makes a fine lunch, or they're a wonderful way to start a hearty dinner.

Here is a kind of *cannelloni* you can make with crêpes: If you live in a town where there is an Italian grocery store, buy some Ricotta cheese and Italian sausages.

Boil the sausages for ten minutes, peel them, cut them into long strips, and brown them in a little butter.

Spread some Ricotta on a crêpe. Add a couple of strips of sausage, and shake Parmesan cheese over all. Roll up the crêpe, and lay it in a shallow baking dish.

(If you can't get Ricotta or the sausages, substitute fine-grained cottage cheese and thin strips of sautéed ham.)

When you have filled your baking dish with rolled crêpes, pour a tomato sauce over them. There's a number of good tomato sauces you can buy, but if you want to make your own here is one:

Chop finely a clove of garlic and a small onion, and sauté them in a couple of tablespoons of olive oil. Add a can of solid-pack tomatoes and ½ teaspoon of basil, and simmer for forty minutes. Add a can of concentrated tomato paste, and simmer for fifteen minutes more. Now strain this and, if it is not good and thick, reduce it for a few minutes over a brisk fire. Be careful not to let it scorch.

On top of the sauce (which is now over the crêpes, remember), shake more Parmesan and some newly ground black pepper. Heat in a 375° oven until the dish bubbles and is pleasantly brown on top. Very fine indeed.

Now for the promise about the leftovers:

The first thing to do in almost all cases is to make a good white sauce: In the top of a double boiler melt 3 tablespoons of butter, add 3 tablespoons of flour, mix, cook a minute, then add gradually three-fourths of a cup of chicken broth and three-fourths of a cup of cream. Stir this till it begins to thicken, then add 3 tablespoons of Parmesan cheese, salt and pepper. Stir until the cheese is all melted and the sauce is creamy.

So, in the icebox you have—chicken?

Chop it up, salt and pepper it, and if you have maybe some slivered almonds or left-over mushrooms, add them. Now mix in 3 or 4 tablespoons of the white sauce, just enough to bind the mixture. Spoon this onto the crêpes, roll them, and line them up in a buttered baking dish. Pour the rest of the sauce over them and bake in a 375° oven till they bubble.

Ham?

If you can steal a few cooked chicken livers it helps. Chop them up with the ham, bind with the white sauce, and proceed as above.

Vegetables?

This seems a fairly elaborate method of getting rid of left-over peas, say, but you can if you want. The method is the same as above.

Egg whites?

It's possible you might have some egg whites in the icebox. Beat four of them till they are stiff. Fold in very gently a half cup of the white sauce, to which you have added an extra tablespoon of cheese. Now be careful. You had better do this next step right in the baking dish. Spoon some of the mixture onto a crêpe, and lightly fold the sides of the crêpe over it. Do not roll tightly. When you have finished your row of crêpes, sprinkle all with more Parmesan and the veriest dash of cayenne pepper.

Do not put any additional sauce over this. Bake in a pre-heated 350° oven for 15 minutes. If you have been living right, you will then have a soufflé inside a crêpe. Good luck.

Tuna fish?

Forget the sauce. Mash up the left-over tuna with a hard-boiled egg. If it's too dry, add a dash of olive oil. Roll the mixture in the crêpes, line them up in a baking dish, and spread over each one a spot of anchovy butter (anchovy paste or mashed anchovy fillets mixed with soft butter: 1 part anchovy to 3 parts butter). Bake these until they're hot.

Anyone here have any left-over *foie gras* and truffles in the icebox?

Purée the *foie gras* with a little cream. Chop the truffles and mix with the purée. Spread on crêpes and roll up: the crêpes themselves *must* be hot. No running in the oven. Serve at once. This recipe, by the way, is pure hearsay.

You get the idea. Shrimps, sweetbreads, crabs, lobsters, all can be used with the white sauce. Just remember to chop things up well.

DESSERT CRÊPES

✳

Dessert crêpes are made from exactly the same recipe as entrée crêpes, except that one tablespoon of sugar replaces the salt in the mixture. There is no difference, of course, in the baking.

Here let us insert a note on blazing. To "blaze" means to pour a couple of ounces of *warm* brandy or other liqueur over the crêpes (which of course are in a flame-proof dish) and setting a match to it. This produces a pretty blue flame and adds a pleasant flavor to the crêpes —and incidentally gets rid of the alcohol.

For some reason a good many people shy away from this operation. They don't mind working around a barbecue-pit which often takes on the aspect of a blast furnace, but the small blue flame worries them. Well, don't let it. Just try it once (with a pitcher of water handy if you are really timid) and you will see that nothing but good results.

Let us begin the fillings with a chocolate cream: Melt a half pound of semisweet chocolate in a pan, then pour it into a bowl, add four tablespoons of butter and 4 egg yolks. Beat smooth, and chill.

Roll some of this up in your crêpes, arrange on that flameproof dish, sprinkle some toasted slivered almonds over all (you can buy the almonds in a can, by the way), and dust with fine granulated sugar. Now pour on the warm brandy and blaze. Do this, of course, at the table. Or you can run the dish under the broiler flame just long enough for the sugar to glaze if you don't want to use the brandy.

Or make a filling of pastry cream: In a pan put half a cup of sugar, three-eighths of a cup of flour, and the yolks of four eggs. Beat this up. In another pan heat two cups of milk with a piece of vanilla bean until it boils. Then pour the milk (take out that vanilla bean) over the flour mixture, beat well, place over a low flame, and keep stirring until the cream thickens to about the consistency of mayonnaise.

This is a good mild cream to stuff the crêpes with. Proceed as above with almonds and sugar—and blaze or glaze.

This cream is also fine in combination. Crumble up some macaroons in it. Or chopped candied fruit. Or fresh chopped strawberries. Or raspberries. Or apricot jam. (Apricot jam, incidentally, is fine mixed with the chocolate cream.) If you are blazing, you may want to experiment with a flavored liqueur—cherry, almond, orange, or whatever.

Bar-le-Duc jelly for some reason is one of the very best stuffings you can find for crêpes. And applesauce—either plain or mixed with pastry cream—is surprisingly good.

And almost any fresh fruit, chopped very well, is good alone or mixed with whipped cream. Try things out, see which flavors you like best.

It's not a bad idea to bring five or six different fillings to the table along with the crêpes and let each guest roll his own. In this case, forget the blazing or glazing. The thing to remember is that the crêpes must be warm. At the table the perfect and traditional utensil is a chafing dish. An electric skillet will work equally well.

Well, now, crêpes Suzette.

There are, of course, dozens of variations for the sauce, but here is a good one: Into a skillet (or the bottom pan of a chafing dish—it is usual to make this sauce at the table) place 5 tablespoons of butter and 4 tablespoons of sugar—these should be creamed together beforehand— the finely grated rind of an orange, the juice of that orange, and half a cup of Grand Marnier or Cointreau (or better, a combination of the two and one teaspoon or less of lemon juice). Stir this sauce thoroughly and bring it to a boil.

Put one crêpe into the boiling sauce. Spoon the sauce over it, to be sure it is soaked. Then fold the crêpe in quarters and push it aside. Repeat until all the crêpes have been poached.

Finally, pour over them a half cup of warm brandy and set them ablaze. Serve each crêpe with a little of the sauce left in the pan.

And that's it.

Good eating. Try not to burn yourself.

* 4 *

PASTA

*

Y̲ou ask a question and you get an answer.

I was in Italy not so long ago, staying on Ischia, a craggy, round, civilized little island—one of those suburbs of pleasure that stand in and around the bay of Naples.

Someone told me to go to Forio, a town on the western coast, and I went. It is a pretty port, with a mountain behind, pink and white villas scattered amiably here and there, and a long sandy beach. It was October, the tourists had gone, there was nothing to do, but it was warm, the views were good, the wine was good, and so was the food.

The food was better than good. At least it was where I had all my meals, in Fillipo's *ristorante*.

Fillipo's is an exceptional place. It is small—bulging, I don't suppose it would hold more than thirty or forty people—it opens onto the beach, and it is owned by Philip Dakin, an American, and Franca, his Italian wife.

Philip and Franca's story is one of those unusual ones you run into quite often abroad. He was an actor in New York—you might have seen him with Helen Hayes in *Happy Birthday*—who one day about ten years ago found himself in the remarkable position, for an actor, of having enough money to take a trip around the world on a freighter.

He set out. Two or three weeks later he went ashore in Italy, and that was the end of the freighter—and the world. With the first step onto Italian soil he felt at home. This was it and he stayed.

For a while he got jobs around Rome making movies; then one spring, when he was on location in Ischia, he met Franca and married her.

Franca Sachetti belongs to one of those large, exuberant, close-knit happy Italian families that own houses and uncles and nephews and vineyards and cousins and sisters and nieces. Philip married them all.

Franca is that marvel, a natural, brilliant cook. Philip knows a great deal about food, so they opened a restaurant. Franca's brother Jocko, who is an artist by daylight, tends the bar when the sun goes down. The place has been a success—in the guest book you will find the names of everybody from W. H. Auden to Burt Lancaster.

I used to go in for lunch late, and eat it on the terrace, over the sand, with Franca and Philip and whatever stray nieces and sisters happened to have stopped by. It was there, one yellow afternoon, that I put my question to Franca.

Franca speaks English well, under pressure, and considering the state of my Italian, she spoke it to me all the time. We were talking about America. She had been there, Philip had taken her on a six-months trip a few years back to meet his family. She loved Wisconsin, his home—although the temperature seems to have stayed at eighty below the whole time she was there—but she knew the rest of the country too: They had driven to Los Angeles and spent the last month in New York. She talked, however, of Wisconsin, only of Wisconsin.

So I asked her the question. "But what about Los Angeles, and New York?" I said. "Didn't you like them?"

Franca hesitated. She glanced at Philip and then she looked out to sea. "No," she said.

"But why?" I said.

Franca hesitated again. She is polite, and after all I was a guest in her country.

But finally she looked up at me. "Because," she said firmly, "because in Los Angeles and New York *there is nothing to eat . . .*"

"She means," Philip said, not quite sure whose side to be on, "she means she didn't like the spaghetti."

I swallowed, but I suppose I looked unconvinced. "Surely there were other things . . ." I said.

Franca rapped her knuckles on the table. "If the

spaghetti is not good, nothing else matters," she said, and then she pointed a finger at me. "You talk a lot about cooking and eating," she said. "Do you know how to make spaghetti?"

"Well . . . ah . . . " I said.

Well, it turned out I didn't.

Franca nodded. "Tonight I will make spaghetti and also noodles, and I will give you a lesson . . ."

"Pasta is the glory of the Italian cuisine," someone is sure to say, and he will be right. Italians eat it at least once and sometimes twice a day, and they have reason. It is wonderful.

Its making, its cooking, its sauces are all matters of great concern to everybody, from the mama of the poorest family to the chefs of the great restaurants. Actually, the preparation is not overly difficult, but there are certain rules—and they are as rigid as those that govern the making of a soufflé—which must be followed.

There are, of course, plenty of people here in America who know how to make spaghetti, but there are, to make an understatement, plenty who don't. It is to them that I—who was lately one of them—address myself.

I sat around Franca's kitchen that night and other nights, and later, in Rome, I sat around a number of other kitchens. I picked up, I think, some tricks of the trade, and also twelve and a half pounds.

Italians, by the way, say that if you drink water, not wine, with spaghetti, you will not gain weight. That's what they say. Don't believe them.

SPAGHETTI

*

In the first place to make spaghetti, or any other kind of pasta, you have to have a big pot. Actually not just a big pot, but a *very* big pot—one that holds two or three gallons.

You fill the pot with water, toss in one tablespoon of salt per gallon and bring to a violent boil. Then you put in the spaghetti, unbroken.

For four people, use a little less than a pound if this is to be a separate course. If it is the main dish, use more, depending on the sturdiness of your clients.

Now comes the all-important and the imprecise direction. No one can say exactly how long to cook spaghetti. The time varies with the kind of spaghetti you use. Some imported from Italy will take as long as fifteen minutes, some American will take no more than four or five. The brand and the size of the spaghetti regulates this. You can't make a rule for yourself and set a clock. You have to stand over the pot and taste.

Spaghetti should be neither hard nor mushy, but at that beginning point of softness when it still resists the teeth.

You must simply fish out a piece, bite it, and decide on the perfect moment for yourself. Only experience will teach you.

When the moment has arrived, immediately take the pot off the stove and drain the spaghetti well in a colander.

Then take out of the oven a large bowl which has been heated there; not just warmed, *heated*. Into it pop a good lump of butter, and splash the spaghetti on top. Then with two forks lift and drop the spaghetti (*never* stir it) until it is well coated with the butter. Now you are ready for whatever sauce you have decided on.

But you must have also made two other things ready: heated plates and eager guests. Like a soufflé, spaghetti will not wait; it must be hot and eaten at once, or it will die.

SAUCES
✳

The things you can put over spaghetti are endless—from anchovies to zucchini. In America there is generally a poverty of choice—meatballs and tomato and that's it. But if you will experiment with some of the following sauces, you will find, I think, the variety rewarding. Quantities given in the following sauces are about right for one pound of spaghetti.

PARMESAN CHEESE, PLAIN

Serve the plates of hot spaghetti with extra butter and a dish of grated Parmesan cheese to sprinkle over them. This is about the simplest and one of the best ways to serve any pasta. But for it the spaghetti must be perfectly cooked and the cheese the choicest. Do yourself a favor about Parmesan. Buy a chunk of it and grate it yourself. The flavor will be noticeably different from that ready-grated in a jar. The best Parmesan is four or five years old.

TOMATOES

Peel three or four medium-sized tomatoes. Chop them up fairly fine. In a saucepan or a skillet melt 3 or 4 tablespoons of butter, add some ground pepper and a little salt, and a bit of basil or orégano, and in this simmer the tomatoes gently for ten or fifteen minutes—until they are cooked but not a mush. Ladle this over the spaghetti at the table and provide a dish of Parmesan as well.

This is the tomato sauce you find often around Naples. You can vary it by adding a minced onion or (for the last few minutes of cooking) some chopped pimiento.

One thing to remember about sauces: Always have them about ready *before* you cook the spaghetti.

FRESH CLAMS

Clam sauces are better in America than in Italy for the good reason that our clams are better.

For each serving buy six or seven fresh clams. (I am speaking, of course, of quahogs—cherrystones or little necks.) Have the fisherman open them and save all the juice in a container. When you get home cut the clams with a kitchen scissors into smallish pieces. Do this in a bowl for the cutting will give you more juice.

In a pot heat a quarter of a cup of olive oil—this is for four people—throw in three or four crushed cloves of garlic, and fry until the garlic is golden. Then remove the garlic and add at least a cup and a half of clam juice. If you haven't that much from your clams, add the necessary amount from a bottle. Now add a handful of chopped Italian parsley and a good grind of black pepper.

You bring all this to a brisk boil, and add the chopped clams. Now watch the clock. For this is to continue cooking only *forty-five seconds*. The clams are not to be boiled, just heated.

With this sauce, spaghettini—which takes only about four and a half minutes to cook—is excellent. Lift the spaghettini directly from the colander in which you have drained it (forget the butter) into hot soup plates, ladle this sauce over it, and bring it roaring hot to the table.

If you can find some crushed Italian pepper to sprinkle over finally, it adds. So does a bottle of cold white wine— but to drink, please, not to add to the sauce.

CANNED CLAMS

For four people you will need a couple of cans of minced clams. Drain the juice from the clams and proceed as above.

A good variation with canned clams is to forget the garlic and, instead, chop up three or four little green onions and cook them a bit in the oil. But do not discard them, leave them in the sauce.

MEAT

This is a rich sauce, one of the endless variations of *bolognese*.

Cut up six strips of bacon and fry them in a skillet. In a couple of minutes add two finely chopped medium onions. When this has browned, add a half pound of ground hamburger and push it around so that it browns, then a quarter of a pound of chopped chicken livers, and do the same. You will find you will need some extra butter for this—a tablespoon might do it, but possibly more.

Peel and chop a large ripe tomato, add it, a touch of salt, and plenty of ground black pepper.

Over this pour a cup and a half of stock—consommé is what you will probably use. Cover the skillet and let the sauce barely simmer for a good half hour, preferably longer.

Serve this over hot buttered spaghetti with, of course, a dash of Parmesan, and you will have a lusty meal.

ANCHOVY

This is more a flavoring than a sauce. Heat a couple of tablespoons of butter and the same amount of olive oil in a pan, fry in it two crushed cloves of garlic until golden brown—no longer—then discard them. In a mortar pound six anchovy fillets, add to the hot butter and oil, and cook gently for a few minutes. Pour over hot buttered spaghetti. You can, of course, use anchovy paste instead of the fillets. About a tablespoon should do it—or more, depending how fond you are of the taste of anchovies.

MUSHROOM

In a skillet melt a quarter of a pound of butter. If you can find some shallots, mince three or four of them, if not, mince a medium onion, and stew gently for a few minutes in the butter. Meanwhile mince a pound of fresh mushrooms—stems and all, very fine—and add to the skillet. Cook slowly and stir frequently. This will take quite a long time, almost one hour, for the mushrooms must be cooked and reduced. Add a little salt and a grind of black pepper at the end, and serve over hot buttered spaghetti. Serve Parmesan separately.

PEAS

This is a dish I find rather mild, but the Italians are mad for it. Their peas, I grant you, are wonderful, small, sweet, tender.

The recipe is certainly simple enough. Cook small fresh peas in a little water until just tender, drain them, and pour over hot buttered spaghetti. Parmesan on the side, of course.

CARBONARA

There seem to be as many ways to make a *carbonara* as there are Italian cooks. But the results are essentially the same: eggs with ham or bacon.

In this case bacon: Cut up eight strips and fry them in a skillet. You may like to use Canadian bacon. If so, cut each slice into four pieces and fry in a good quantity of butter—you must have hot grease left in the pan.

Separate four eggs. Stir the yolks lightly with a fork.

Now, when you have drained the spaghetti and dumped it into the hot bowl, pour over it the bacon and the hot grease. Lift and mix with forks. This must be kept very hot, for now you pour over it the raw egg yolks and lift and mix again. There must be enough heat to set the eggs. Give it a good grind of black pepper and serve with Parmesan. Right tasty.

If you want to, you can use the whole eggs instead of just the yolks.

TUNA FISH

For a seven-ounce can: Break the fish into small pieces, and heat it in a pan with a couple of tablespoons of butter. Pour over it a scant cup of hot chicken broth, give it a grind of black pepper, and let it simmer a few minutes. Throw over it some chopped parsley if you like.

Alternately, instead of the chicken broth, use a scant cup of hot cream. This is very good.

Serve with Parmesan.

Incidentally, on the subject of fish, there is a kind of canned bouillabaisse imported from France which you will sometimes find in fancy food stores. If you will use about half the amount of water which the label calls for, heat it well and pour it over spaghetti, you will have a surprising and very good sauce.

And if you like sardines, you can make a most acceptable sauce by using the tomato-onion recipe above and breaking up into it a can of sardines.

P E S T O

This is quite a lot of trouble but good if you can manage it. You will need first of all a mortar and pestle.

Into the mortar put one cup of fresh basil leaves, one clove of garlic, a dash of cayenne pepper, a dash of salt, and 2 tablespoons of pine nuts. Begin pounding. Add gradually a quarter of a cup of grated Parmesan cheese. When this has turned into a thick mess add, a little at a time, 4 to 5 tablespoons of olive oil. The consistency should be something like very soft butter. For four. If you have a blender, dump everything in at once, and run for thirty seconds.

A tablespoon of this—you don't heat it, by the way— over hot spaghetti is something you will remember.

C H E E S E   A N D   C R E A M

Rich and easy.

Over the hot buttered spaghetti in the bowl sprinkle a quarter of a cup of Parmesan. Lift and mix this with forks. Grind over it some black pepper. Then pour over it a good half cup of *hot* heavy cream. Mix again and serve with some more Parmesan. Actually, this sauce is best on noodles.

WITH TRUFFLES

Sprinkle hot buttered spaghettini with a half cup of Parmesan, lift and mix. Then lay over all a couple of very thinly sliced white Italian truffles.

You will have to buy these in a can—they are rare but not impossible to find. If ever you are in Italy in the winter, ask for fresh ones. You can eat them on anything, from slices of turkey to slices of toast, and they are spectacular. And if you are flying home, put a couple in your pocket—as a present for me. Please.

A COLD SAUCE

Here is an absolutely excellent dish which Franca made for me one hot noontime, and which, the chances are, you have never even heard of.

Peel a couple of ripe tomatoes and mince them. Seed a sweet green pepper and mince it. Do the same with three good stalks of celery. To all this add 2 tablespoons of capers and a little fresh or dried orégano and basil. Add salt and a generous grinding of black pepper.

Put this all in a glass jar. Sprinkle a few drops of vinegar over it, and then pour in just enough olive oil to cover. Set it in the icebox. It should stay thus at least four hours—longer if possible—until it is good and cold.

When you are ready, serve the spaghetti—not buttered—on individual hot plates (everything must be extra hot this time) and then ladle over it the cold sauce. No cheese.

CHICKEN LIVERS, COLD

Buy a half pound of already cooked and seasoned chopped chicken livers from a delicatessen. Refrigerate until good and cold. Then put a tablespoon on each portion of hot buttered spaghetti.

TARTARE

To a half pound of raw hamburger add a raw egg, a finely minced smallish onion, lots of pepper, and enough salt. Mix it all up with your hands. Refrigerate.

Use a heaping tablespoon over each portion of hot buttered spaghetti.

Variation: If you can find a couple of tablespoons of caviar, mix it into the *tartare*.

Above all, do a little experimenting. Mix things. Add mushrooms to peas. Fry some thin slices of zucchini in butter and throw that over the spaghetti. Add chopped parsley to practically anything. Or more herbs. The thing to do is to find or invent sauces you like, and not limit yourself to meatballs and tomato paste.

NOODLES
✳

In Italy noodles are used interchangeably with spaghetti. So, all the sauces above will work equally well on a dish of good noodles.

They are cooked in the same way: in much too much salted water and drained the instant they are done. There is no exact way to time them, either. You can get them just right only by trial and (probably) error.

You can buy, of course, perfectly good noodles, but without too much trouble you can make better ones.

Try to lay hands on some unbleached flour, but if you can't, regular will do.

Into a bowl break four eggs and add a tablespoon of olive oil and a teaspoon of salt. Beat this up a little and add flour. You will need two and a half to three cups or maybe more, but just how much more depends on the kind of flour. Anyway, make a good stiff dough and knead it until you have a cohesive ball. Keep flouring your hands and the board. However, don't overdo the flour.

When this dough is ready, divide it into four or five

parts, and roll each one out. You will have to keep flouring the rolling pin. Each piece must be rolled out *very* thin, until it handles like silk. When this has happened, fold each piece several times and cut with sharpest scissors or knife into the desired width. **Dry on a towel for a** couple of hours before using.

All this can be done with practically no trouble at all **if** you buy yourself a noodle-making machine. This is an elegant little contraption that reminds you of an old-fashioned clothes wringer in miniature. It rolls out the dough for you and then cuts it—in two sizes—all with the twist of a handle.

* 5 *
EVERYTHING
BOILED

*

My first lesson in the art of French cooking
came about by accident. It was a long time ago, I did not
write down the recipe because I had no idea then that I
would ever get involved in cooking, but I have not forgotten it. The place was Algiers, the time during the war, in
1943.

What a relief it was to be in Algiers. I had lately been
bound down in Washington—oppressed by security, and
lieutenant-colonels, and standing up straight, and being on
time, and saluting, and making five copies of every sort of

nonsense, and saying yes sir, and—well, life in the Pentagon. Algiers was a revelation.

You could get up at a decent hour, read the papers at breakfast, wear comfortable clothes, salute nobody (except, I suppose, General Eisenhower, but he never came around my part of town), and in the main carry on like a rational human being.

I lived, for a while, in a dreary ancient hotel near the Aletti, but then, through a piece of luck, I found an apartment of my own. It was on the top floor of a house on the Michelet, and it was something pretty fine. It had a living room, a bedroom, a kitchen, and a bath, and while it was somewhat expensive, it was worth every cent I paid, for in the living room there were, aside from the usual number of chairs and sofas and tables, six life-sized white marble statues of Venus in assorted poses. They weren't very *good* statues of Venus, they looked to have been done in the 1890s; but that's a detail, there they were: six life-sized statues of Venus. You don't find that in many living rooms. I settled down very comfortably.

The concierge of this apartment house I will have to call Madame X, for to tell the truth I do not remember her name. She was a Parisian who had lived in Algiers for some years; she was a formidable dame with a large front, black clothes, and a face that was weary and efficient. We did not become friends immediately.

She got me a man to make my bed and clean the apartment. A man: Yameni Mohammed looked about fourteen but was actually seventeen, a thin, bone-thin, ugly little

Arab boy who spent half his time out on my balcony looking down at the traffic.

He was a trial, at first. When not on the balcony, he was
constantly chattering, constantly under foot, and he spoke
a French that was not my French. This made him im-
patient with me, of course; when I would not understand,
he shouted, then pointed, and finally hit his head with his
two fists at my stupidity.

I tried. I became aware that one word recurred constantly in his conversation. It sounded something like
Zhan-jay Ro-jay. He wanted to know, it occurred to me,
if, in America, I was acquainted with Zhan-jay Ro-jay. I
could only shrug.

But then one day, his worn sandals flapping on the tile
floor, his dirty white burnoose swinging awkwardly, he
danced a kind of Arab jig. And he screamed, *"Zhan-jay
Ro-jay, Zhan-jay Ro-jay."*

Lightning struck. Ginger Rogers. Did I know Ginger
Rogers?

I was about to say no when I remembered that before
the war I had once been at a party in California where
Ginger Rogers was, and that I had actually shaken hands
with her. "Yes," I said. "Yes indeed." I knew Zhan-jay
Ro-jay.

It was the turning point in our relationship. I became
the respected American. Yameni Mohammed suddenly
understood my French and I his. I invented a long series
of glamorous meetings I had had with Miss Rogers not
only in Hollywood but New York as well. Exhausting

97

work, for I had nothing to go on. Once, just to vary things, I said I also knew Rita Hayworth, but Yameni was not interested. No. To this poor, strange, starved little Arab boy there was but one dream of beauty, one loveliness unexcelled, one light in the world—Ginger Rogers.

Miss Rogers has given me a great deal of pleasure through the years, but never more than in that icy winter of 1943.

The friendship of Madame X was a little harder to come by. Being French, she understood that the abstract ideal had its place, but something more practical was needed to move her. Especially in that weather.

I got my hands on a mason jar full of anchovies, I don't know how. I intended to eat them myself, naturally, but they were so salty I could not get even one down. I soaked them in cold water for a couple of days, but it did no good, the black salt taste remained. I gave them to Madame.

Well, a couple of nights later as I was coming in, she stopped me and thanked me.

"Were they good?" I said.

"Delicious," she said and for the first time she smiled.

This gave me an idea. My apartment was so cold that you could not take your overcoat off except to go to bed. *But* it had a fireplace. Was there any way she could find me some wood?

Actually there was. Madame was a friend of the mayor of Algiers, and it might be possible that, for a price, something could be arranged.

When I came home the next night the wood had ar-

98

rived—cork logs and neat little bundles of kindling. Madame was in my apartment, instructing Yameni in the art of building a fire.

Cork logs are hard to start, but finally they caught, and we stood around, the three of us, admiring the blaze. I took off my overcoat for the first time in days.

It was an occasion. I had some bottles of white Algerian wine, I opened one, and we drank. At least Madame and I drank, Yameni would not, so I gave him my most cherished possession—a Mr. Goodbar. This was a concoction of peanuts and chocolate which the PX rationed as if it were fresh caviar and which I firmly believed to be the best thing I had ever put in my mouth. I remember I vowed in those days that if I ever got home I would never be without a Mr. Goodbar, and in fact the first day I arrived in America I bought a box of forty-eight. Well . . .

The wine was good. In that strange, cleaned-out city of Algiers, there was nothing to buy in the stores, nothing, except wine and flowers. But the wine was excellent. It was made by monks somewhere back in the hills—those same Trappists who make the excellent Oka cheese and grow the famous Oka melons in Canada. They made a fine brandy, too, aged eight months, and once at Christmas I gave a party at which we had Old-Fashioneds made of it, trimmed with a cherry Life Saver and a slice of tangerine. Quite good.

So we celebrated. The black-out curtains kept out the black night, and the fire cast a surprising tint on the marble flesh of the six naked Venuses. We talked politely, I

99

am sure. A foreign language tends to act as a barrier that blocks out anything that is not polite and good.

But suddenly the sirens sounded and we had an air raid.

In a minute the guns began and we crowded out on the balcony to watch. With Eisenhower up at the St. George Hotel, the city was of course crawling with anti-aircraft pieces, they sprang into action from every roof top, there seemed to be, literally, hundreds of them. Let us hope no one will ever again be able to witness such a display: but hundreds of thousands of tracer bullets cutting the black sky make a breath-taking sight.

No planes got through that night, there were a few bombs dropped, but Yameni's experienced ear said they had gone into the ocean. Suddenly there was silence, then an all clear, and we went back to the fire.

Madame said something to Yameni in Arabic, he answered, they talked for a moment, and then she turned to me to explain.

It would be possible, she said, for Yameni to obtain a good amount of fish—since the bombs had dropped in the sea—and if I liked, she would make bouillabaisse for dinner tomorrow night.

I was not as enthusiastic as I should have been. "You mean you'll make it out of dead fish?"

"Not dead, no. The fish are stunned by the detonation of the bombs, and it is easy to pick them from the surface of the water."

I must still have looked skeptical, for Madame spread her arms and said, "What does it matter how a fish dies, so long as it is fresh?"

Of course, that made perfect sense, so I said yes, wonderful, let's have bouillabaisse.

A few small arrangements had to be made, naturally. If Yameni were to be out to sea at the first light of day to pick up the fish he would need a boat. Luckily some vague relative of his owned a boat which could be hired for a very few francs, and Madame, for only a very few francs more, could perhaps obtain a salad and perhaps an onion and, and . . .

It wasn't much.

I was home early the next night, seven o'clock, for I did not go to my mess. The apartment was warm, there was a fire not only in the living room but the kitchen as well. The stunned fish, now definitely dead, were cleaned and laid out prettily on a table. And there were onions and tomatoes and eggs and something that looked like coffee but unhappily turned out not to be—well, a feast.

I put on some dry clothes (it was raining, of course) and went back to the kitchen to watch. Madame had brought up a big black pot with a lid from her kitchen, she had knives and other tools and some professional looking bowls. I wandered around with a glass of wine in my hand and felt high-toned and useless. Yameni had washed his burnoose, I noticed. It was a party.

Madame began. She cut the larger fish in pieces, the smaller she left whole. She cut a couple of onions in four, did the same to three or four little tomatoes. She cut four thin slices from a lemon, another four from an orange. All of this went into the pot. She added olive oil, quite a lot. She uncorked a bottle of white wine, poured the whole thing into the pot. Then she added enough water to cover everything. Salt and pepper, of course, and some other stuff which I didn't know about then but do now—but the above list is the essentials.

Then she put the pot on the hottest part of the stove, and said, "In twenty minutes we eat."

In twenty minutes we ate.

First I ate plenty, then I ate too much, then I stuffed myself. The Luftwaffe had done us well, there was enough, more than enough, for everybody. We had a long loaf of coarse bread to sop up the juice, we had salad to give us a feeling of respite, we had more of the wine, we had a fire. A memorable dinner.

And it was a dinner. We had a dessert. Madame had found some eggs. She beat them up a little, poured them into a skillet, turned out an omelet. When it was on its plate, she sprinkled sugar on it, then warmed a little cup of brandy, poured that over and lighted it. What a dessert. You never had anything better, anywhere.

The coffee, no. But you can't have everything.

I remember, from that evening, only one piece of conversation. It is pat to my purpose, but it is fact, not fiction, and fact is always more pat than fiction.

"Who would ever have thought," I said, "that a boiled fish could taste like this."

Madame looked at me over her napkin, over her front, through her old, weary, knowing eyes. "To boil is the best way," she said. "Everything. When you boil you do not lose one particle of goodness. If only I had a piece of beef . . ."

It was many years before I had that bouillabaisse again, but then suddenly I did—and here is the recipe, from Ruth Norman, who got it from a fisherman of the island of Port Cros, off southern France, just across the Mediterranean from Algiers:

Buy three pounds of stunned fish—cod, halibut, or whatever is really fresh, but be sure you include a couple of small ones you can use whole. Buy also a dozen fresh clams and a dozen uncooked shrimps.

Put the fish, properly cleaned and cut, into a big pot.

Add four slices of lemon, four of orange.

Add a pinch of saffron, salt and black pepper, a half dozen cloves, a clove of garlic, chopped, a touch of thyme, and a handful of chopped parsley.

Add two large onions, quartered, and two large tomatoes, quartered.

Pour in a cup of olive oil, a bottle of *good* dry white wine, and then enough water to cover the fish.

Bring all this to a fast boil and keep it boiling for no more than twenty minutes. The clams and the shrimp should be added for the last five minutes only.

Serve this in big soup bowls with hot French bread to sop up the juice, and you will not regret it. Serves 4.

Now to get back to Madame X's fortuitous remark: One fall *The New York Times* asked a half dozen of the most famous chefs in the city what they ate on their days off. To a man they gave one answer: boiled beef.

Learn a lesson from this: These masters of the high cuisine, these men who command an endless supply of cream and truffles and pheasants, they eat, when they get a night off, boiled beef.

So, remembering what Madame X had said, I began to collect recipes for all kinds of boiled foods: chicken, beef, veal, fish. While maybe she exaggerated in saying that boiling was the best way to cook, it is certainly one of the better ways. And a change.

So:

BOILED BEEF

Buy a four- or five-pound piece of brisket of beef. Get more than you'll need, in other words. (This is more than *I* need.) It's very good cold.

Put the meat in a heavy pot that has a lid that fits tightly. Surround it with a couple of stalks of celery with the leaves left on, an onion stuck with four or five cloves, a teaspoon of powdered thyme, a handful of chopped parsley, (3 tablespoons) and, of course, salt and pepper.

Now cover with water and bring to a fast boil. Reduce the heat to simmer, and skim off the scum that will have formed.

Clap on the tight lid and let the beef cook for two and a half hours. Test it with a fork. The chances are it will not be done, but at the end of three hours it should be.

Here are the classic vegetables for a boiled beef: cabbage, potatoes, leeks, onions, carrots, white and yellow turnips, parsnips. You will want to use the potatoes and two or three of the others. Now if you are a great expert and know from the looks of them exactly how long each vegetable will take to be done when the beef is, you can simply add them to the pot. But the chances are you don't know, so the best way is to cook each of your vegetables separately in some extra beef broth. You want them done but not overdone.

To serve this, you need large soup plates. Put a slice of beef in each plate, surround it with the vegetables, and then pour some of the broth, strained, over all. Serves 6-8.

Then eat in good health with a horseradish sauce:

Whip a half pint of heavy cream, then fold in a teaspoon of freshly grated apple and a tablespoon of freshly grated horseradish. If you can't get fresh horseradish, the bottled kind serves, but drain it well.

For the New England variation of this, proceed exactly as above, with this addition: Cut a half pound of lean salt pork into cubes and boil it with the beef from the beginning.

For the French *pot-au-feu*, you proceed also as above, except that an hour and a half before the beef is done, you add a chicken. A three- or three-and-a-half-pounder will do, cut in half to fit more easily into your pot. Serve everyone a slice of chicken and a slice of beef. Serves 8.

The Italians make a dish called *bollito misto*—boiled mixed meats. I have "adapted" it, shall we say, because a real *bollito* calls for a calf's head, and I somehow don't see you split-level gourmets rushing to the local supermarket demanding calves' heads.

In a large kettle put a piece of beef brisket—four pounds. More than cover it with water. Forget the vegetables and the seasonings, except the salt and pepper.

An hour and a half before the beef will be done, add a chicken, cut in two. An hour before, add a couple of veal knuckles or calves' feet or both, also a good-sized piece of pork sausage (in its casing, of course).

When the meats are done, pile them on a big hot platter. No broth this time. Give everybody a slice of everything, and serve a variety of hot sauces—peppery hot, I mean. In Italy you always get *salsa verde*, which is made of olive oil, lemon juice, a couple of cloves of garlic, chopped, some drained capers, salt, plenty of ground black pepper, and lots of chopped parsley.

This is a fine dish, by the way. Serves 6-8.

Here is one of the great beef boils. It is called in France (and everywhere else) . . .

BOEUF EN DAUBE

In your heaviest pot with the tightest lid put: a half pound of butter; 3 tablespoons of olive oil; a quarter of a pound of salt pork, diced; six or eight pepper corns; two cloves of garlic, chopped; a good shake of salt; a small can of tomato paste; and 1 teaspoon of thyme, 3 tablespoons of chopped parsley, and a ring of orange peel.

Now on top of this four pounds of top round in one piece. On either side of this put half a calf's foot. Pile in a pound of small white onions, peeled, and four or five medium carrots, sliced.

Now (are you still with me?) over all pour a bottle of the best red wine; Châteauneuf-du-Pape will do, but be sure it is of a good year. The wine *must* be excellent.

Bring all this to a fast boil, reduce heat to a simmer, and take off the dark scum that has formed. Then clap on the lid and simmer very slowly for five or six hours, turning the meat twice.

Serve it with boiled new potatoes or buttered noodles, with plenty of grated Romano cheese and right out of the pot. I can't wait. Serves 8.

CAPE COD TURKEY

Now an ancient Cape Cod winter boil. It is called Cape Cod turkey, but it is made, naturally, with cod fish.

Cut up a couple of pounds of salt cod and soak it for six hours, changing the water twice.

Peel a dozen medium onions and four medium potatoes, and peel and dice four beets. Boil each of these separately till they are tender.

In a skillet render a half pound of diced lean salt pork until the bits are well browned. Remove the bits and with

2 tablespoons of the drippings make a white sauce—2 tablespoons of flour, the drippings, a cup of milk, salt and pepper.

Now, in fresh water, poach the cod for fifteen minutes, drain it, put it on a hot platter, surround it with the vegetables, and pour the white sauce over all. Finally, sprinkle with the salt-pork bits.

It's good, it's cheap, and you can find everything you need to make it down cellar. At least Cape Codders can. Serves 4-6.

BOILED LAMB

Into a large heavy pot put a couple of onions, sliced thin, and two carrots, sliced thin. Add salt and pepper and 3 good tablespoons of butter. Heat this to bubbling, and then in it brown a leg of lamb. Be sure the lamb will fit into the pot—have as much of the bone cut off as possible and, if there are chops on the leg, probably they must go too. Or do you have a large pot?

When the lamb is browned, pour in enough *good* white wine to half cover it. Stir in also a tablespoon of tomato paste and two cloves of garlic, chopped. Put on a tight lid, set the pot on a back burner of the stove, and simmer it for five or six hours. You may find that you will need a little extra wine. Well, add it, for the lamb must always be in bubbling liquid. Also turn the leg several times.

This lamb, when served, is not cut with a knife but

dolloped out with a spoon. Skim the fat from the liquid left in the pot; strain the liquid and use it as a sauce. Broiled tomatoes and glazed onions accompany this dish well.

And now veal, or to give it its proper name . . .

BLANQUETTE DE VEAU

For four people, into that same old heavy pot put two pounds of veal shoulder, cut in cubes. Cover with water, bring to a boil, skim off the scum, lower the heat to a simmer, and add: twelve tiny peeled white onions; a half cup of thinly sliced carrots; a clove of garlic, chopped; and a pinch each of thyme, salt, and freshly ground pepper. Put on the lid and simmer for an hour and a half. At the end of an hour, add a cup and a half of chopped mushrooms.

About ten minutes before the meat is done, make a sauce—in a double boiler—of 1 tablespoon of butter, 1 tablespoon of flour, and a cup and a half of the liquid from the veal. Heat until thickened.

In a bowl beat together three egg yolks, a tablespoon of lemon juice, and a cup of cream. When this is smooth, pour it into the double-boiler mixture. Now stir constantly over low heat until all is hot and creamy.

Drain the veal, pour over it the thick white sauce from the double boiler, and then sprinkle over everything a handful of finely chopped parsley. Very, very good.

Well, there are a hundred other things to boil, from haggis to *truites au bleu* to corned beef and cabbage.

All you need is that pot, some clear cold water, and the desire—the desire, as Madame X said—to preserve "every particle of goodness."

* **6** *

LEMONS

*

Away to make a friend is to find someone who shares a common passion: Bird watchers like other bird watchers, Giant fans like other Giant fans (at least they used to), people who crawl around in caves like each other, Weimaraner owners are all pals (if you can believe the Weimaraner magazine), Yale men are forever getting together, and so on and so on down the line, a process of natural selection.

I have recently made a new friend, a girl who shares with me a passion for lemons. I suppose there are a great many people who could belong to such a brotherhood, but I have run into only a few of them—devouts, that is, who feel uncomfortable if there are not at least a dozen lemons in the icebox.

This is how it happened. An old friend one night took me to an unobtrusive little restaurant: Unobtrusive is right; it was in a cellar, it had no liquor license, its décor was, shall we say, serviceable. The waiter, however, was friendly, he brought us icy glasses for the wine we had drug along, and he spread out before me a menu which had on it a notable item: lemon soup.

I had lemon soup. Had I ever had it before? I half remembered that I had, at the Grande Bretagne in Athens, but I couldn't be sure, I have a bad memory.

But here was this: It was white, it was smooth, it looked creamy but was not creamy, and it was brillantly loaded with lemon. It was fine.

After that a broiled chicken. And a dish of rice which had a lot of things in it, particularly a squeeze of lemon. Then a salad of artichoke hearts, marinated properly in oil and, need I say, lemon juice.

"What kind of food is this?" I said.

"Greek."

To me Greek food had always been something stuck on a skewer and something else wrapped up in grape leaves. I was never sure what; if I guessed lamb it often turned out to be eggplant. You must have had that experience.

"But . . ." I said.

"Come on," my friend said. "I'll introduce you to the cook."

So I met Christine.

Christine was not my picture of a Greek cook. She was young, she was lovely, and at that moment she was standing in front of her stove in a little black dress and a huge, white, stiff, starched chef's coat that fitted her like a Balenciaga—it was inches too big, everywhere.

"How do you make that soup?" I said.

"Nothing to it," said Christine.

Until recently Christine had belonged to that happy band of restaurant gypsies who live by following the sun, the jobs, and their inclinations. It was in Key West, for instance, that she met her husband, Ralph Martell, who had a little bar there. When they were married, they went to the Virgin Islands. After a year of that they jumped to Cape Cod—and so on, until finally, because what they really wanted was a place of their own, they came back to New York.

After the standard, endless delays, they managed to open the Café Briki and Christine found herself, with a fork in one hand and a lemon in the other, mistress of her own kitchen at last. She had always known the cooking of the Peloponnesus, where her family came from, so it was decided that the menu should be essentially Greek. But since she is American and sensible, her steaks were great and you didn't have to experiment with a *bourekakia* unless you wanted to. But you wanted to.

I went often to the Briki, lugging my wine with me and I learned, simply by asking, how Christine dealt with a lemon.

The soup, to begin with: In a pot pour six cups of chicken broth. Boil this, and add a third of a cup of rice. Boil now for fourteen minutes.

While that is going on, beat two eggs in a bowl—better in an electric mixer, it makes it easier—then squeeze a half cup of lemon juice and add to it a half cup of the boiling broth.

Now—the only hard part—add the lemon broth to the eggs, *slowly* and beating constantly. They must not curdle.

When you have accomplished this, add the egg-lemon mixture to the rice broth, stir, and you have your soup, for four or maybe six.

Very good and even better cold. Try it cold sometime, followed by an anchovy soufflé, p. 21, and a chicory salad. You will have a meal.

The artichoke salad: Buy a couple of boxes of frozen artichoke hearts, cook them as you are told on the box, drain them well, and cool them.

Slice a half dozen scallions very thin, add them to the artichokes. Add some fresh dill if you have it, otherwise a bit of dry. Get this mixture very cold. Then stir in, some time before you are ready to eat it, a dressing of four parts oil and two parts lemon juice, with ground black pepper and plenty of salt. Serves 3-4.

Here is something to put over broccoli: Make a white sauce: 2 tablespoons of butter, 2 of flour, cook a minute or two, add a cup of milk, and stir constantly until it is very thick. (Much easier in a double boiler.)

Add a dash of nutmeg, and salt and pepper.

Stir together a cup of chicken broth and a half cup of lemon juice, then pour slowly onto three well-beaten eggs, stirring *constantly*. Add this to the white sauce, with maybe a couple of tablespoons of freshly grated Parmesan cheese. See that the whole thing is hot, of course, and you have something fine for broccoli. Or if you know how to stuff cabbage, it is good over that.

The old friend who first took me to Christine's, Rogers Brackett, is actually the father of the lemon cult, and my guide and mentor. Let me illustrate:

A few years ago he was in Florence. He spent a day at I Tatti, and after Mr. Berenson had filled him with books, pictures, food, and conversation, he took a turn around the gardens.

Now in the gardens of I Tatti there are lemon trees. They were, at that moment, bearing. My old friend without thinking twice about it, pinched a dozen lemons from Mr. Bernard Berenson.

The final handshakes were accomplished with bulging pockets, but no matter; Mr. Brackett descended into Florence, that night took a train to Paris, and a few days later the *Ile-de-France* to New York.

Are you aware that it is forbidden to bring lemons into this country? Are you aware that lemons—ten days picked —smell violently like lemons? "Violently?" my old friend says. "I smelled like Scarlett O'Hara's mother."

Well, maybe there is a kindness in the customs service —the lemons from I Tatti arrived at 54th Street.

117

Now Mr. Brackett has a grocer, and the grocer, to finish the story, is a Florentine. Mr. Brackett took two of his lemons and gave them to the grocer.

And the grocer, a man long parted from his city beside the Arno, held the lemons in his hand and, with his voice and eyes a little extranatural, said, "You have brought me the sun!"

Mr. Brackett makes a veal like this: For two people, buy a pound of veal, sliced paper thin. Flour it a bit and then pound it paper thinner. Salt and pepper it, then sauté it, a few pieces at a time, in lots of butter for not very long, remove it, and keep it hot.

Add to the skillet a large dash of white wine, scrape up all the bits, and reduce the mixture to half. Pour over the veal.

Now, sometime before, you have sliced a lemon into slices so thin you can read through them. Eat the veal with the cold lemon on top, rind and all.

Here are a few other lemon dishes:

SCALLOPS WITH LEMON

For four people, get two and a half pounds of *sea* scallops. This is a surprise, you do not need bays.

Spread them out in some sort of baking dish—a big Pyrex one is sensible—squeeze over them the juice of two lemons, dot them with butter or a few squirts of olive oil, and grind over them plenty of black pepper. Then let them sit for a couple of hours. This is very necessary.

To cook, put them under the broiler for twelve or fifteen minutes. When they are browned they are done. Poke them or turn them once as they cook. You will be pleased at how good they are.

A LEMON CHICKEN

Brown a cut-up fryer in butter in a skillet for which you have a cover. When it has reached the proper golden tone, pour over it a half cup of lemon juice, reduce the heat to the lowest flame, put on the cover, and let the chicken simmer for three quarters of an hour. This will serve three or four people.

A LEMON FISH

Buy a three-pound piece of the freshest fish you can find. Lay it in a shallow baking pan, pour a tablespoon of olive oil over it, salt and pepper it, squeeze a clove of garlic over it with a garlic press, and then completely cover the fish with thin slices of lemon.

Bake in a pre-heated 350° oven for thirty or thirty-five minutes. Make some parsley potatoes to go with this.

It will serve four generously.

✳ *Cook Until Done* ✳

FONDUE BOURGUIGNONNE

This recipe is really a ringer among the lemons, but it tastes good.

You need an electric skillet for this. You put it in the middle of the dining room table, and everyone does his own cooking. First of all you must buy the best beef—really *nothing* but fillet will do. Trim off all fat and cut the meat into approximately one-inch cubes. Buy half a pound or a little less for each person.

Bring the beef raw in a bowl to the table. Supply each guest with a number of very thin pats of plain butter. Have your electric skillet hot and make each guest work: He melts a pat of butter and then on the end of his fork cooks his own cube of beef until it is done as he likes it. Now, as a seasoning for the beef you serve a variety of other, prepared butters. First among these is lemon butter:

Squeeze the juice of a whole lemon onto a quarter of a pound of soft butter. Mix well and mold the butter again into a nice shape in a little dish. Keep it in the icebox until you are ready to use it.

With this beef you must have more than just lemon butter—you want anchovy butter, parsley butter, herb butter. Actually, anchovy is the important one.

You make these in approximately the same way you make the lemon butter. Strength to taste.

120

This lemon butter is good over vegetables. Cucumbers for example:

Peel three ordinary-sized cucumbers, cut them into about half inch slices, boil these in a little salted water for seven or eight minutes until they are soft, drain them, and then smear over them a good tablespoon of the lemon butter.

This will serve four. You can do zucchini the same way.

RICE SALAD WITH LEMON

Mix two cups of cooked white rice with a tablespoon of olive oil, the juice of a whole lemon, and salt and pepper. Now stir into it a tablespoon of mixed chopped chives, parsley, and dill, plus one raw cucumber which you have peeled, seeded, and chopped fine. This will serve three or four.

You could do exactly the same thing with cooked black-eyed peas, cooked chick peas, or for that matter plain potato salad.

LEMON ICE

After a heavy meal there is nothing better.

If you know how to make lemon ice, make it. Otherwise do what I do, buy it.

Serve each guest a portion in some likely looking dish

and then, here is the secret, squeeze the juice of half a fresh lemon over each portion.

Easy, simple and excellent.

Or don't you like lemons?

* **7** *

REPERTOIRE

*

I know a girl called Solveg who has the right idea.

I met her by chance. A friend of mine called me up and asked me to come to dinner to meet his cousin. Now if there is one thing I have learned in a long life it is never to go to dinner to meet anybody's cousin, so I must have been trapped into this. In any case, I went.

Solveg was a dandy surprise. She was young, she was blond, she was exceedingly pretty, and she was doing the cooking. Or so she said. She wandered around the apartment with a wooden spoon in one hand and a martini in the other, chattering amiably, but only very occasionally going into the kitchen to give something a poke. I remember I paused to wonder once or twice about what we were going to have, because no matter what gentilities may be in store, I like to eat first.

I need not have worried. In time she brought forth a beef Stroganoff, and an excellent one. There was a great deal of it, too, and a salad and a bottle of wine. I ate and ate.

Well. Solveg has some vague job with a music company and it turned out, later, that she had a tape I wanted to hear. So it was arranged that I was to come around to her house the next week for dinner and a listen.

I went. And after the same scene with the wooden spoon and the martini, she brought forth—a beef Stroganoff.

"Good," I said. "You remembered how I liked it."

"I must tell you something," Solveg said. "Beef Stroganoff is the only thing I know how to cook. I mean that. I cannot cook anything else. Not anything. Nothing."

"How come?"

"I do not believe in cooking at my age. But my mother insisted I learn how to make one dish in case of emergency."

"Emergency," I said, "what emergency?"

"The only emergency," she said, pouring out the wine. "When I am not taken out to dinner."

"Ah," I said.

"A girl has only a few years to get taken out. When she is thirty, I should think, it is all over. *Then* is the time for the gracious life to begin—making hollandaise and all that horror."

"I guess you're right," I said.

"It is a very bleak prospect," Solveg said, "to think you will have to spend all your time in the kitchen with wild rice and chicken breasts. I refuse to anticipate it."

"You have a point."

"I know a hundred restaurants in New York. Any one of them is preferable to home. Some are more preferable than others, of course. Chambord, for instance . . ."

"All right," I said. "Next time I'll take you out."

"Good," Solveg said. "Still, Mother was very wise. I think everyone should know how to make one dish."

It was a phase of cooking that had not occurred to me. Yet there must be thousands of people who normally blanch at the sight of a skillet but who would—secretly perhaps—like to be able to cook one thing.

So we have arranged a one-dish repertoire: none is very difficult, yet each will give the impression that you know what you are doing. Beef Stroganoff, I might add, is not among them. I've had enough of that.

Someone once said that money cannot buy happiness, but that is, I believe, a cynical remark when you consider this first dish.

It is a dish for a man to make. I had thought to recommend it to lechers, but that is hardly necessary: any man who makes it, adds a simple salad and a bottle of champagne, will automatically *be* a lecher.

✳ *Cook Until Done* ✳

At first sight this may seem complicated but actually it couldn't be simpler.

FILLET OF BEEF
WITH FOIE GRAS

You are planning to serve eight for dinner. Buy a four-pound short loin fillet of beef and a lavish amount of *pâté de foie gras* (at least four ounces). Have the butcher prepare the beef—trimmed of hard fat and tissues. Heat your oven to 450°, then roast the fillet in it for twenty five minutes. When it is done, take it out and slice it almost through; you should have eight slices.

Between the slices spread a liberal amount of *foie gras,* then push the fillet back together again, and place it under the broiler just long enough to get hot.

If you want to be fancy you can serve this with some frozen artichoke hearts (the directions are on the package) and some small whole fresh or canned potatoes, browned in butter.

And you really should have a béarnaise sauce to serve over the fillet. Here's how you do that.

Cook together:

> 1 *cup tarragon vinegar*
> 1 *tablespoon dried tarragon*
> 1 *tablespoon finely chopped onion or shallot*
> ½ *teaspoon salt*
> *Dash of black pepper*

128

You must boil this until it is reduced by one third. Now strain it into the top of a double boiler. Now beat the yolks of six eggs and add them to the vinegar. Melt a half pound of butter and pour it slowly into the egg-vinegar mixture, beating constantly. You don't want this sauce to boil, just heat, so watch out. If you like you may add a dash of cayenne or Tabasco.

VITELLO TONNATO

3 lbs. veal cutlet
1 qt. dry white wine
2 small cans tuna fish in oil
12 anchovy fillets
2 cloves chopped garlic
3 sprigs parsley
¼ cup olive oil
1 sour pickle, cut up
1 chopped onion
Salt and pepper to taste

For the sauce:

Pan juices
2 tablespoons lemon juice
2 tablespoons mayonnaise
2 tablespoons capers

Have your butcher slice two cutlets from across the leg and flatten, roll, and tie them. Put the meat in a pot which is just large enough for it and which has a tight cover. Add all of the above ingredients except those for the sauce.

Bake, covered, at 350° until tender—about two hours. A meat thermometer will read 170°. Let cool in the pot, then remove the meat to a platter, and slice. Strain the juices from the pot, beat in the lemon juice and mayonnaise, add the capers, and pour over the veal. (Or you may blend the pan juices, unstrained, with the lemon juice and mayonnaise in your blender, and then add the capers to the sauce.) Serve cold, but not too cold.

Garnish the platter with hard-boiled egg halves, tiny pickles, and water cress, and serve with a dish of hot rice. Serves 6.

An idiot could make this:

SPARERIBS AND
SAUERKRAUT

3 *lbs. spareribs*
3 *lbs. sauerkraut, fresh or canned*
4 *apples*
4 *potatoes*
1 *cup water*

Wash and drain the sauerkraut. Peel and slice the apples and potatoes—thick slices. Put a layer of sauerkraut in the bottom of your roasting pan. Then a layer of apples, top them with kraut, then the potatoes, more kraut, season with salt and pepper, and then on top of all of this, place the spareribs. Pour on a cup of water, cover, and bake in a slow oven, 325°, for three and a half to four hours. The ribs should be tender enough to munch. Serves 4-5.

DOUBLE LAMB CHOPS
WITH BAKED POTATOES
AND BROILED TOMATOES

In case that idiot doesn't like sauerkraut, here is something else for him/her.

Right on the broiler rack place as many double lamb chops as you will need with as many tomatoes cut in half as you will want and a suitable number of large mushroom caps.

Light the broiler.

Shove your lamb chops, etc., under the flame—not too close—and after about five minutes take a look to see if the chops look done. If they do, turn them over and brown them well on the other side.

When they're finished, put everything on a warm platter and take it to the table.

Of course this is the simplest possible way. If you would like to be a touch fancier, you might chop a few onions finely and spread them over the tomatoes—which, by the way, in any case should have a dot of butter upon them.

As for the baked potatoes, wash as many as you need, rub them with bacon grease, bake in the oven, 350°, for an hour. You have to start them first, of course.

When they are done, split them and stuff in a big hunk of butter.

Let everyone do his own salt and peppering.

TROUT POACHED IN
WHITE WINE

6 *trout—the frozen kind comes two to a package that sells*
   for less than a dollar
2 *tablespoons butter*
1 *medium onion, or 3 shallots, chopped*
2 *cups dry white wine*
Salt and pepper
2 *tablespoons flour*
½ *cup heavy cream*
2 *tablespoons chopped parsley*

Melt the butter, sauté the onion in it until limp, place the trout on this, and add the wine and some salt and pepper. Bake the fish in a hot oven, 450°, until done (flaky), about ten minutes.

Remove the fish to a hot platter. Mix the flour with enough water to make a paste and add it to the liquid in the pan. Now cook this, on top of the stove, until thickened. Then add the cream and parsley and reheat. Finally pour the sauce over the fish. Serves 4-6.

CHICKEN BREASTS IN CHAMPAGNE SAUCE

2 large chicken breasts
6 tablespoons butter
1 tablespoon oil
1 cup champagne
1 teaspoon lemon juice
2 tablespoons cream
Salt and pepper
¼ cup chopped parsley

Have your butcher bone two large chicken breasts; cut them in two and flatten somewhat. Brown them on both sides in the butter and oil, then cook them for fifteen minutes, uncovered. Remove them to a hot platter. Add the champagne and lemon juice to the fat in the pan, and cook until this mixture is reduced by half. Then add the cream and heat, don't boil, the sauce. Season with a little salt and pepper. Pour over the chicken and sprinkle with the parsley. Serves 4 meagerly.

Of course drink the rest of the champagne with this.

SUKIYAKI (WITH RICE)

1 lb. sirloin of beef, cut into paper-thin strips
1 onion, sliced thin
1 bunch scallions, sliced

133

¼ cup sherry
½ cup beef broth
*¼ cup Japanese soy sauce (**Kikkoman is a good one**)*
½ tablespoon sugar
1 cup bamboo shoots, sliced thin
2 cups mushrooms, sliced thin

If you have an electric skillet, this is a good—and a good-looking—dish to do at the table. If you haven't, well, use a regular skillet. But it must be large.

So: Heat the skillet and grease it with a tablespoon of oil. Add the onions and stir; add the meat and stir until it is seared on both sides. Then push the meat to one side, add the sherry, the beef broth, the sugar, the soy sauce, and the bamboo shoots and mushrooms, and stir-fry for about four minutes.

Make rice for this. You will find directions on any box of it. And, of course, have some clear tea. Serves 4.

ROAST DUCK WITH A
BIGARADE SAUCE

Wipe the duck (five or more pounds) with paper towels and sprinkle the cavity with salt and pepper. Prick the skin.

For roasting, the simplest thing to do is this: Remove the broiler pan and its rack from the bottom of your stove, place the duck on the rack, and put the whole thing into the oven. (If you can't do this, be sure you roast the duck on a rack in a *shallow* pan. There must be low sides.) Cook now for three hours in a slow oven, 350°.

For the sauce: When the duck is done, put it on a hot platter, or better still put it in another pan and leave it in a warm oven. Then remove the rack from the roasting pan and skim off the fat you will find in it. Frankly, you will have to remove a good deal of that fat.

Now, on top of the stove, over very low heat, stir into your remaining drippings about a teaspoon of flour or cornstarch. Add 2 teaspoons of sugar and 1 tablespoon of wine vinegar.

Stir all this up and add the juice of an orange and of a half a lemon.

Again blend all of this, and add three or four thin strips of orange peel and about a tablespoon each of grated orange and lemon rind.

Unless you are an expert you had better slice the duck breasts and disjoint the legs in the kitchen. Arrange on a hot platter.

Now, finally, pour over the sauce and decorate your platter with some water cress. Serves 4.

CASSOULET

4 *cups white beans (the canned variety), drained, or if you can't find them canned, soak 2 cups dry ones overnight*

2 *lbs. breast of lamb, cut up for stew*

½ *lb. coarse sausages (Italian or Polish), sliced ½ inch thick*

½ *lb. lean bacon, cut up*

2 *large onions, chopped*

2 *tomatoes, chopped*
1 *clove garlic*
Bread crumbs
Butter

First: Cover the lamb with salted water and simmer until tender, approximately an hour. Drain the meat and reserve the liquid. Take the bones out of the lamb.

In a skillet brown the sausage lightly in butter. Remove it and put it in the bowl with the lamb. Cook the bacon in the same skillet. When it is crisp, remove it and put it too with the lamb.

Now in the bacon grease cook the chopped onions for a couple of minutes, add the chopped tomatoes, and cook until the tomatoes are soft. Pour over these vegetables the water in which the lamb was simmered.

Rub an earthenware casserole with garlic. Into the bottom of it put the meats—the lamb, the sausage, the bacon. Over that put the four cups of white beans. On top pour the onion, tomato, lamb-water mixture.

Now sprinkle with bread crumbs and dot with butter. Grind some black pepper over all.

Put this in a 350° oven and bake for an hour. (If you have used soaked dried beans, the dish must stay in the oven for two and a half hours.)

All you need to eat with this is French bread and red wine, a salad and cheese—and maybe a chilled pear.

And by the way, this dish is even better if it's a couple of days old. Simply take it out of the icebox, let it return to room temperature, then heat in a moderate oven for about twenty minutes. Serves 6-8.

M O U L E S   M A R I N I È R E

This is a dish you can have only if you live along the coast and can lay your hands on a quantity of mussels.

Let's say this is a recipe for two people: Buy four pounds of mussels.

These must be thoroughly scrubbed—with a stiff brush, and no kidding. If you have bought any whose shells are open, throw them away.

In your best-looking iron pot—which you can bring to the table—put the mussels, pour over them a couple of cups of good dry white wine, and add a pinch of thyme, a handful of chopped parsley, a clove of garlic, chopped, and a couple of tablespoons of chopped onions or, if you can get them, shallots. Put in also a couple of tablespoons of butter and a good dash of freshly ground black pepper. Now put the pot over high heat and let it cook until the mussels have opened. This shouldn't be more than five or six minutes.

Bring the pot to the table and serve the mussels in soup plates. You use your fingers to eat, naturally, and you sop up the wine with big hunks of fresh French bread.

I said this would be enough for two people, but it's not really. Double everything.

* 8 *

THE EGG

*

Of all the provender that man in his long peculiar history has decided to swallow—from birds' nests to Brie—eggs are without any question the most versatile.

You get up in the morning, read *The New York Times*, and conclude the world is coming to an end; you sit around at midnight, secure with a drink in the notion that all considered life is a pleasant business: and what do you eat? An egg. In the morning you want it spartan, boiled; at midnight you don't mind if it is bubbling in a champagne sauce or maybe stuffed with *foie gras*.

And you will eat anybody's egg: a turtle's, a plover's, a sturgeon's, a turkey's, a shad's; but most of all you will eat a hen's.

A hen's. Think of it. Is it not surprising that a hen—the most stupid and irritating of living things—should produce such a prize? Such beauty: nature's most elegant envelope, framed in so fearful a symmetry that even Brancusi must pale at the sight of it, and filled with a meat that—well, you've had eggs, command your own superlatives.

Here now follows a cycle of eggs, from morning till midnight. Although on the whole easy enough to prepare, eggs are not a docile food, they require your constant attention, they have almost without exception a critical moment, and you must be around to seize that moment.

EGGS FOR BREAKFAST
✳

So far as anything fancy is concerned: in the morning, no. A sensible person will not trust himself with anything so hazardous as a knife before eleven o'clock, so save the chopped up mushrooms and the peeled tomatoes for later. The following recipes can be made with only one eye open.

BOILED EGGS

This is the best way: Put your eggs in a pan, cover them with cold water, set them on the fire, and let them come to a boil. Then turn off the flame and let them sit in the hot water for one minute. This makes them about perfect. Alexandre Dumas says to use beef bouillon instead of the water, but I can't think what that would do.

FRIED EGGS

These are always a hazard, but here are a few hints: First use a skillet that has a lid. Melt a pat of butter in the skillet, drop in the eggs, then flick a few drops of water off the end of your fingers onto them and put on the cover. Keep the heat low. Take a look every now and then and when they seem done take them out. If you can be trusted at this hour to find the vinegar bottle, pour a couple of drops into the remaining hot butter and swirl it around until the mixture is black, then pour it over the eggs.

POACHED EGGS

Fill the skillet half full of water, bring it to a boil, then turn down the flame until the water is barely simmering. Break each egg into a saucer, then slide it carefully into the water. When the eggs appear set take them out with a slotted spoon and plump them on buttered toast. If you find you have trouble with the eggs sticking to the skillet, try greasing the skillet a little before you put the water in. And if some morning you feel even worse than usual, use milk instead of water, and eat the toast and eggs in a soup plate with the milk poured over them.

SCRAMBLED EGGS
WITH BACON

In a skillet put a pat of butter, melt it, and then lay in three or four strips of bacon. When the bacon is cooked, take it out and pour off almost all of the grease. Put the skillet back on the fire, turn the flame very high for about a minute, then turn it off. Now pour in the eggs which you have beaten very lightly—hardly more than just mixed them—and swirl them around in the pan with a fork. The instant they are set—this operation shouldn't take more than thirty seconds—scoop them out with a spatula.

144

SHIRRED EGGS

In a small round shallow ovenproof dish melt a pat of butter, then break into it a couple of eggs, shake some salt and pepper over them, and put them in the oven. A slow oven—about 350°. It will take longer than you think for the whites to set, but keep watching them, you don't want the yolks overcooked.

THE LAST RESORT

Let us not forget the Prairie Oyster. On that unhappy morning when your head is only too evidently but sounding brass and a tinkling cymbal and feels as if it had been removing mountains, try this: Into a champagne glass break an egg. Salt and pepper it. Douse it with Worcestershire Sauce. Put the glass to your lips and, with one gulp, swallow.

If it stays down, you will live.

EGGS FOR LUNCH

✳

There are a million, but let's start off with cold ones.

But first a couple of words on eggs *mollets,* for they will be used in many of the recipes. You start off eggs *mollets,* as you would boiled eggs, in cold water, bring to a boil, then turn off the heat and let them lie in the hot liquid for three minutes. You then take them out and plunge them into cold water. In fact, keep water running over them until they feel completely cold. Now comes a slightly delicate operation. You must gently crack these eggs and peel them. The shells will not come off easily, as the shells of hard boiled eggs do, so take care. Now:

EGGS IN ASPIC I

For these you need ramekins.

Into a cup of cold bouillon, chicken or beef or a mixture of the two, empty two envelopes of plain gelatin. Let this soak for three or four minutes, and in a saucepan heat three more cups of the broth and empty the gelatin mixture into it. Give this a stir and set it aside to cool.

When it is cool put a tablespoon of the gelatined broth into the bottom of each ramekin and let this harden in the icebox. When it is jelled place on top of it a round of something you like, *prosciutto* perhaps, or cooked ham, or *pâté de foie gras.* Or you can make a design with tarragon leaves or slices of black and green olives. Then on top of this put the egg *mollet* and fill up the ramekins with the remaining broth.

Then into the icebox until they are hard set. This will take three or four hours.

You can eat them either as they are in the ramekins or turn them out onto a plate. They make a fine first course.

EGGS IN ASPIC II

This is much the same as the above, except you use a ring mold instead of the ramekins. Make the bouillon and the eggs *mollets.* Rinse a ring mold in cold water, swirl a bit of the broth around it until it has begun to set, then place the eggs in the mold and insert something between them—a slice of *foie gras,* or maybe a rolled anchovy fillet—then cover with the rest of the broth.

Give this plenty of time to set—four or five hours in the icebox, and when you are ready to use it, dip it for just an instant in hot water and unmold it on a platter.

Surround it and fill the center with something—small leaves of lettuce, cherry tomatoes, slices of cucumber. Serve it with a sauce made by thinning mayonnaise with a little heavy cream and a tablespoon of fresh lime juice.

While we are speaking of eggs in aspic, let us not forget roe. An extremely good way to begin a lunch—or a dinner, for that matter—is with shad roe in aspic. This is simple enough: Buy a couple of pairs of shad roe, poach them in a skillet or a saucepan of water, to which you have added a little lemon juice, salt and pepper, and maybe a slice of onion, until they are done—about ten minutes. Then drain them, put them in a bowl, rip off the outer membrane, and separate them lightly with a fork. Put them into a ring mold and pour over them chicken broth to which you have added two envelopes of plain gelatin as advised above. This must be allowed to harden, of course, and then unmolded and garnished in the same way as the egg ring above, and served with the same thinned mayonnaise.

(Incidentally, if you like jellied consommé, a pleasant thing to do with it is to swirl a couple of teaspoons of either black or red caviar into each soup-cupful before the consommé has jelled.)

OTHER COLD EGGS

Buy a couple of cans of tuna fish, mash them up, and mix them with a couple of tablespoons of good mayonnaise. Make this into a mound in the center of a platter, surround the mound with as many eggs *mollets* covered with tartar sauce as you will need. Of course, make some decorations with water cress and slices of tomato.

The variations on such a dish are infinite. For instance, in the asparagus season center your platter with cold asparagus in a vinaigrette sauce, surround it with eggs *mollets,* and then cover the eggs with a *chaud-froid* sauce. *Chaud-froid:* In a cup and a half of chicken broth you soften and dissolve two envelopes of plain gelatin. You then make a white sauce—3 tablespoons of butter melted in the top of a double boiler (oh, the problems a double boiler solves in making white sauce) with 3 tablespoons of flour added, blended, and cooked a bit. Into this you pour a half cup of cream and the cup and a half of gelatined chicken broth. Stir constantly until the sauce is thick, then take it off the stove and cool it. When it is cooled, you spoon it over the eggs. Let the whole thing set in the icebox.

Or you can make a platter of eggs *mollets* sitting upon artichoke bottoms. Where do you get artichoke bottoms? You buy them in a can, eight of them for something less than a dollar. Of course, you must cover the eggs with something, a *chaud-froid*, or spoon aspic over them, or a thinned out mayonnaise, or tartar sauce.

HARD-BOILED EGGS

The best thing to do with a hard-boiled egg is to take it out on a beach, crack it on your head, and eat it with salt and a bottle of ice-cold beer. But barring that ideal circumstance, here are some other things to do with it.

1. Halve the hard-boiled eggs, take out the yolks, mash them with either red or black caviar, add a dash each of fresh lime and onion juice, a little salt and pepper, and pile that mess back into the whites.

2. Do the same thing with the yolks and a small can of sardines plus lemon juice, a tablespoon of mayonnaise, some chopped parsley, and salt and pepper.

3. Or mix a small can of ham spread, a couple of tablespoons of chopped chutney, and a dash of onion juice with the yolks.

4. Or chop up some celery and a couple of sweet pickles, add a dash of vinegar, a tablespoon of mayonnaise, and salt and pepper, and mix with the yolks.

EGGS WITH ANCHOVIES

Here's a good beginning with hot eggs. Hard-boil a half dozen eggs, peel them, cut them in two lengthwise, and take out the yolks. To these yolks add three or four mashed anchovy fillets, or about a tablespoon of anchovy paste, and also a little cream—enough so that when you beat this all up you have a fairly liquid mixture. Put the halves of egg whites in a shallow baking dish, spoon the anchovy mixture over them, and run them into a medium oven until they are bubbly.

Now, some rather more substantial dishes which will do for the main course at lunch.

The first is:

QUICHE LORRAINE

I hesitate to include a *quiche* because it calls for pastry, and pastry requires a really expert hand. If you do not know how to make a pie shell I recommend you to page 414 of Mildred Knopf's *Cook, My Darling Daughter*. Follow her recipe for incomparable cream cheese pastry and your troubles will be minimized. Anyway, line a nine-inch pie pan with one-quarter-inch-thick rolled-out pastry dough. Do not pre-bake it. On the bottom lay narrow strips of either Swiss or Gruyère cheese. Criss-cross these with strips of crisp bacon which you have cooked in butter. Now in a bowl beat together four eggs, some salt, a dash of cayenne, and two cups of light cream. Pour this over the cheese and bacon. Cut a couple of tablespoons of butter into small pieces and dot the top of the *quiche* with them. Sprinkle with a tablespoon of minced parsley.

This now goes into a preheated 375° oven and it is

cooked until it is lightly browned on top which will be almost forty minutes. Take it out and let it cool. In about half an hour it should be right to eat. Serves 4-5.

PIPÉRADE

Chop two ripe tomatoes, a green pepper, a clove of garlic, a tablespoon of parsley. Put them in a skillet with a tablespoon of butter and one of olive oil. Add a half teaspoon of celery salt, a half teaspoon of salt, and a dash of pepper. Cook these slowly until they are very tender and the liquid from the tomatoes is cooked away. Stir in then five eggs lightly beaten and let them set—but only just. The eggs should not be fried hard. Slide the whole thing onto a hot platter. Serves 3-4.

EGGS FLORENTINE

These can be made without much trouble any more because you can buy creamed spinach frozen in a cellophane bag. So, buy a couple of these bags, prepare them according to directions, and then dump the contents into a shallow baking dish. Poach eight eggs, and when they are done, drain them, and carefully arrange them on top of the spinach. Then make a rich white sauce: 2 tablespoons of butter, melted and mixed with 2 tablespoons of flour—in a double boiler—with a cup of cream, a cup of chicken broth, and a half cup of grated Parmesan cheese added; stir until you have a thick, smooth mixture. Pour this over the eggs, sprinkle with a little more Parmesan, and shove the dish into the oven until the top is slightly brown. Serves 4-6.

WITH BAKED POTATOES

Bake as many medium-sized potatoes as you will need. When they are done—about an hour—cut a hole in each and scoop out the insides. Mash them with some butter, salt and pepper, and a little milk, and then half fill each skin with his mixture. Break an egg into each potato, shake some salt and pepper over it, and add a few drops of either butter or cream. Bake the potatoes in the oven until the eggs are set.

EGGS IN CREAM

Into ramekins pour about a half inch of boiling heavy cream. Then into each ramekin break an egg. Add salt and pepper. Put the ramekins in a shallow baking dish half filled with boiling water, and simmer for a couple of minutes on top of the stove. Put the whole thing into the oven for about three more minutes until the eggs look set. These are messy but good.

WITH TOMATOES

Cut some good-size tomatoes in half, scoop out about a tablespoon from each—enough to make a depression that will hold an egg *mollet*. First bake the tomatoes in the oven for about half an hour, in a baking dish with a little water, until they are soft. Remove from the oven, place an egg *mollet* in each depression, then cover each with the cheese sauce described in eggs Florentine. Then return to the oven until the dish is hot and bubbly.

OMELETS

The professionals would have you believe there is a certain mystique about the making of omelets: There is not, all that is required is a little skill. In the first place, to make a decent omelet you must have a proper pan. You can buy such a pan almost anywhere, it has curved sides, and once you have it, take care of it—never use it for anything else and never wash it; wipe it clean with paper towels.

It is possible to make large omelets, but the best are individual—two-egg—ones. Here is the method: In a bowl break two eggs, add a small splash of water, not quite a

154

teaspoon, some salt and pepper. Now beat these eggs lightly with a fork. I mean lightly—the eggs should be no more than mixed. Heat a pat of butter in the omelet pan. The pan should be hot, but not roaring. Now pour in the eggs.

Here is the moment where a little skill is required. You remember the old game of rubbing your stomach and patting your head? Well, what you do with an omelet is something like that. You rotate the skillet an inch off the fire and with the fork you pull in the eggs from the edge of the pan. Continue this until all of the mixture has come in contact with the hot bottom of the pan, then for just a moment you allow the omelet, untouched, to set.

Now you take the pan, tilt it over the hot plate on which you will serve the omelet, and from the top you begin to roll it. This is easily enough done, the omelet is not hard, you simply roll it up and slide it onto the plate.

That's the plain omelet. You can stuff omelets with almost anything your heart desires. When you do this you merely place the stuffing in a line along the center of the omelet just before you begin to roll it.

What do you like? You can have crumbled bacon, finely chopped onions, creamed mushrooms, Parmesan cheese, diced ham, shrimps, creamed spinach, well—whatever.

The thing to remember is this: Omelets must be made quickly, never allowed to get hard; the surface, in fact, before you roll them should be almost semiliquid, still with a shine—and of course they must be eaten at once. There is nothing docile about an omelet.

And, of course, the old stand-by:

WITH CORNED-BEEF HASH

In a fairly shallow baking dish break up a couple of cans of corned-beef or roast-beef hash. Edge this with half slices of tomatoes, some chopped peppers, and maybe a sprinkling of chives. Put this in a medium oven for about twenty-five minutes and just before you are ready to serve it poach four eggs and lay them on the hash. This serves four very easily and well.

EGGS FOR DINNER
✻

Maybe the best thing you can do with an egg for dinner is to go back and read Chapter I on soufflés, or else let it grow up and become a nice plump, tender chicken. If you do the latter, here are a few ways to attend to it:

FOR A BARBECUE

In a big heavy enameled skillet put a cut up chicken, pour over it a cup of white wine, add a sliced onion, a squeeze of lemon juice, a tablespoon of olive oil, salt and pepper, and a small pinch of rosemary if you like, but better a pinch of tarragon. Now let this marinate, all day if possible, turning the pieces of chicken so they will be well soaked. When you are ready to cook, place the skillet over a low fire and let the chicken stew in its marinade for a good half hour. It will be by this time almost cooked. If you intend to use an outdoor barbecue you need only roast the chicken on the grill until it is well browned and crisp. The same goes if you are cooking it on a rack under the broiler. This method obviates the necessity of long and tedious basting.

BROILED

This is simple enough. Lay a broiler, cut in two, skin side down in a shallow pan big enough to hold it. Squeeze half a lemon over each half and rub all over with plenty of butter. Put extra pats of butter in the cavities, add some salt and pepper. Run the pan under the broiler, as far from the flame as you can get it. Now watch this chicken. Baste with the butter every five minutes

157

until this side is well browned. Then turn the halves over, baste again all over with butter, and broil them until they are a good color.

At this point they may not be quite done, so now put them up above in the oven for another ten or fifteen minutes. Of course, continue the basting.

WITH DUXELLES

Have your butcher bone and cut in two four breasts of chicken. Make mushroom *duxelles* (see p. 65) and stuff the chicken breasts with this. You will find a flap on the inside of the breasts, and you will be able to put about a tablespoon of the mushrooms into this. Arrange the eight half breasts, not too close together in a large shallow glass baking dish. You will have some *duxelles* left over; pile some on each breast. Into the dish pour a cup of chicken broth, squeeze over all the juice of two lemons, and add another couple of tablespoons of butter. Shake some salt over each breast and give each a grind of black pepper. Put this into a 350° oven and baste it every ten minutes. At the end of an hour you will have a superlative dish. Serves 4-6.

À LA VIENNOISE

For this use the breasts and the second joints of four young chickens. The breasts, preferably, should be boned. Make a marinade of white wine—no more than a cup—the juice of a lemon, a touch of olive oil, salt, pepper, some chopped parsley and a pinch of thyme. Let the chicken marinate in this for a half hour or so, turning it, of course.

When you are ready to cook, take the pieces of chicken out, wipe them dry with a paper towel, roll them in flour, shake them off, dip them in a beaten egg, and then roll them in dry bread crumbs.

Now you must have ready smoking hot deep fat, 375°. The fat must be extremely hot, for the point with this chicken is to seal the outside with a crust and not let the fat penetrate to the flesh. Plunge the chicken into the fat, and when it is a good deep brown it will be done. As you take each piece out, drain it, of course, and then pile the pieces on a hot platter. Serves 6-8.

Traditionally this chicken is served with French-fried parsley, but go to some other cookbook to find out how to make that. I never have much luck. I like to eat it with an extremely cold cucumber salad—the cucumbers sliced thin, seeded, and left to wilt in plain French dressing.

CHICKEN HASH

With a sharp knife chop up whatever left-over chicken you happen to have around. But don't bother unless you have enough for at least two cups. Blend into this 3 or 4 tablespoons of heavy cream and about the same amount of purée of *foie gras*. (Purée isn't particularly expensive.)

Now cook some noodles and take them out of the water just before they are done and mix them with butter.

Put the noodles around the edge of a large shallow buttered baking dish, heap the chicken in the center and then grate over all some fresh Parmesan cheese, dot with butter, and brown in an oven. It's not a bad idea to pour a little extra cream over everything.

WITH GRAPES

You can use either a freshly boiled chicken or leftovers, but you need two or three cups of coarsely chopped cooked chicken meat to begin with. Make a very rich white sauce with 3 tablespoons of butter, 3 of flour, a cup of heavy cream, and a cup of strong chicken broth.

Mix this with the chicken, put it into a baking dish, and then cover the whole thing thickly with little white seedless grapes—washed and stemmed, of course. This will take thirty minutes in a 350° oven. Serves 4.

160

COLD WITH MUSTARD

Split young broilers, salt and pepper them, rub them with soft butter, and bake them in the oven until they are done. This is an irritating direction I know, but chickens vary and you will have to find out yourself by testing with a fork. In any case it should take something under an hour.

Take them out, spread them with prepared mustard, sprinkle them not too heavily with some dried bread crumbs, and put them under the broiler for a few minutes until they are nicely finished—that is, until the crumbs are brown. Actually these are very good hot, but somehow they are better cold, served on a slice of ham.

You can do exactly the same thing and achieve quite a different effect by spreading the chickens with a purée of *foie gras* instead of the mustard.

BOILED

No one ever boils chickens. Too bad. They are very good.

Put a chicken in a pot, almost cover it with a mixture of half chicken broth and half beef bouillon. Add to the broth a chopped onion, a chopped carrot, a couple of stalks of chopped celery, and some sprigs of parsley.

161

Boil the chicken gently until tender, take it out, drain it, and serve it with a heavy white sauce made with cream and chicken broth, and flavored with sautéed mushrooms. Needless to say, that's a fine broth you have left there for soup.

EGGS FOR DESSERT
✳

POTS DE CRÈME AU CHOCOLAT

Very easy and very good, but you need an electric blender.

Into a blender dump a six-ounce package of semisweet chocolate bits. Add to this one square (two ounces) of unsweetened chocolate, chopped up a bit. Now heat a half pint of light cream—it must be light—plus 2 tablespoons of milk until it is hot, but not boiling. While the cream is heating, separate four eggs.

Now add a dash of salt to the chocolate and pour the hot cream over it into the blender. Turn on the motor and let the blades go until the racket has stopped and the mixture sounds smooth. Take the top off the blender and slide in the four egg yolks and let the motor go for another minute.

162

Pour now into four ramekins and set in the icebox. About an hour before you will use these pots of cream, take them out of the icebox; they should be eaten at room temperature.

CRÈME BRULÉE

There are two ways to make *crème brulée*. The ingredients are the same for both: eight egg yolks, a quart of heavy cream, two tablespoons of white sugar, and plenty of light-brown sugar.

For the first: In the top of a double boiler heat the cream to the boiling point. In a bowl beat the egg yolks well with the 2 tablespoons of white sugar. Pour the hot cream over the yolks slowly, beating all the time with a wire whisk. Now return all this to the top of the double boiler—you have to have a fairly large one—and, stirring constantly, cook for another five minutes. At this point pour the cream into a large shallow baking dish.

The cream must cool completely. When it is cold put a couple of cups of light-brown sugar into a sieve and shake it over the cream. You want the sugar to be thick, about a quarter of an inch.

Now comes the indignity. You must have had your oven turned on full blast so that the broiler compartment is very hot. You put the cream under the flame and with the broiler door open you get down on your hands and knees and watch what is going on. The sugar will caramelize—that is, it will melt. What you are doing down there on your hands and knees is seeing that the sugar does not burn and is all evenly melted, because the moment it is you must take the cream out of that broiler.

Let the dish cool, then put it in the icebox. It must be served very, very cold.

When you serve it the caramelized surface should be so hard that you have to crack it with a spoon.

For the second method: Behave exactly as you did in the first up until and through the point where you pour the hot eggs and cream into the baking dish.

Then what you must do is put this dish into a pan of hot but not boiling water and shove it into the oven. Well, this is a clear enough direction, but try doing it someday. The baking dish is shallow, the pan with the hot water will necessarily have to be even shallower. So try this. Put the pan *sans* water into the oven, then pour the water in and set your baking dish in it.

Your oven, by the way, should be at 325° at this moment.

Bake the custard until it is done, a half hour will probably do it, but test it. Insert a silver knife into the custard and if it comes out clean it is done.

Take the custard out of the oven, cool it, put it into the icebox until it is completely cold, and then go through the same song and dance with the light-brown sugar and the indignity that is described above.

I wish I could tell you some foolproof method to get rid of that hot water that is still there in that pan. You will probably do what I do. Spill it all over the oven.

CARAMEL CUSTARD

In a small heavy iron skillet or saucepan melt a half cup of sugar, stirring it constantly until it begins to brown. Pour an equal amount of this into six custard cups. Tilt each cup a bit so that the caramel coats the side.

Beat three eggs with a pinch of salt, a quarter of a cup of sugar, and a half teaspoon of vanilla. Now scald two cups of milk, and gradually pour it over the eggs, stirring all the time. Fill the custard cups with this, and set them in a pan of hot water—that again!—and bake for thirty minutes in a 350° oven.

When they are done, chill them.

FLOATING ISLAND

Separate five eggs. Beat the whites until they are beginning to be stiff, then add to them gradually a half cup of sugar and continue beating until they are very stiff.

In a wide saucepan heat a pint of milk with half a vanilla bean. Never let it boil—you had better use an asbestos pad. When the milk is warm, make large nicely rounded spoonfulls of the egg whites and drop them onto the surface of the milk. You probably can't do this all in one batch. But cook each meringue for a couple of minutes on one side and then for a couple of minutes on the other. As they are cooked put them on a platter to cool.

Now beat the five egg yolks with a half cup of sugar, and pour the hot milk over them slowly, beating all the time. (Be sure you still have a full pint of milk. Add some cold if necessary.) Pour this into the top of a double boiler and stir constantly until it thickens, about five minutes. Take this cream off the hot water and chill it. Discard the vanilla bean, of course.

As you see, all this can be done long before you need to use it. So can the final step. In a small heavy iron skillet melt a half cup of sugar and stir it until it is a rich brown. Take it from the heat, add 3 tablespoons of strong black coffee and 3 tablespoons of Grand Marnier, return to the fire, and stir until the syrup is smooth and slightly thickened. You can keep this at room temperature until you are ready to use it, but when the time comes, reheat it and then dribble it over the meringues on the platter.

Serve a couple of the meringues on a plate with the cold custard around and over them.

ZABAGLIONE

For two: In the top of a double boiler beat together four egg yolks, 4 teaspoons of sugar, and 4 tablespoons of Marsala. You have to cook this slowly and beat it constantly. When it thickens pour it out into a couple of nice big champagne glasses. It is a pleasant if somewhat over-rated dessert.

CHOCOLATE BAVARIAN
CREAM

This is synthetic but none the less it tastes all right. Make the *pots de crème au chocolat* as directed above but, instead of pouring it into ramekins, pour the whole thing into a large bowl. Whip a half pint of heavy cream until it is very stiff, and then carefully fold it into the *pots-de-crème* mixture. Spoon this into some likely looking bowl and put the whole thing into the icebox. It works.

BOILED CUSTARD

If you're sick, and who isn't during these hard winters, this is the perfect dessert to have after that broiled lamb chop and baked potato: In a bowl beat four egg yolks with a quarter of a cup of sugar and a pinch of salt. Into this stir in slowly a pint of hot milk. Pour it all into the top of a double boiler and keep stirring until the custard coats a spoon—just a few minutes. Take it off the fire and stir in a teaspoon of vanilla or maybe a little grated lemon rind, then cool it in the icebox. Great, as I said, if eaten in bed with a fever. Or drunk, rather. Use a cup.

THE MIDNIGHT EGG
✳

If you are up at midnight and in the mood for eating, nothing simple will do. Try these:

EGGS IN CHAMPAGNE SAUCE

Chop up finely a couple of medium onions and a half dozen mushrooms. Sauté them gently in 3 tablespoons of butter and add a little salt and pepper. When they have melted sufficiently—about ten minutes—take the skillet off the stove and rub a tablespoon of flour into the mixture. Return this to the fire and cook again for a couple of minutes. Now add a half cup of cream and a cup of champagne. Stir up well until this begins to thicken a little.

This is a good moment to transfer the sauce to a chafing dish (top pan over simmering water). Now lay in the sauce a half dozen eggs *mollets*—or hard-boiled eggs will do—and let them remain until they are warmed. Keep pushing the eggs around gently. Serves 4-6.

Serve the eggs on toast with the sauce over them. Drink the champagne.

EGGS WITH SHRIMP

Chop up a half dozen mushrooms and boil them for five minutes in two cups of chicken broth. Add then three-fourths of a pound of cooked shrimp and three or four sliced artichoke bottoms (*bottoms*, not hearts. You can get them in cans, remember?). Add a good dash of cayenne and some bits of *beurre manié*.

For *beurre manié:* To 1 tablespoon of softish butter add 2 teaspoons of flour. With your fingers work these together. Drop little pieces of this mixture into the broth.

Turn down the heat and, stirring all the time, let the liquid thicken. You can now use a chafing dish and proceed with half a dozen *mollets* or hard-boiled eggs as above, but a good thing is to poach the eggs.

Put each egg on a piece of toast and spoon the hot shrimp stew over it.

EGGS IN EGGS

This is a trick, but it always seems to amaze the simple hearted.

Prepare a cheese soufflé as instructed on page 13 to the

point where you are ready to slide the whole thing into a soufflé dish. That is to say, the beaten egg whites have already been folded into the cheese mixture.

At this point you must have four poached eggs ready. You can have made them a half hour before, there is no particular reason for their being hot, but they must be *dry*. Be sure you drain them on a towel.

Spoon two thirds of the soufflé mixture into the soufflé dish. Then carefully lay the poached eggs in a circle on the soufflé, and cover them with the rest of the mixture.

Cut out four round pieces of cheese—about the size of nickels—and place one directly above each egg, so you will know, when the soufflé is cooked, where the eggs lie.

Put the soufflé into a preheated 350° oven and bake it about eighteen or twenty minutes.

Each serving should be one huge scoop of soufflé, so that each eater will discover an egg in his portion. There will be a lot of headshaking about this, and I can't think why. It isn't all that good.

GOLDEN BUCK

Something simpler?

In a chafing dish, over hot water, melt a tablespoon of butter. Into that dump a pound of grated Cheddar cheese. As the cheese begins to melt pour in a cup of ale. Sprinkle on a half teaspoon of dry mustard and stir and stir until the rarebit is smooth and hot.

Poach some eggs, lay them on toast, and spoon the hot

rarebit over them. Pass the Worcestershire and drink lots of cold ale *avec*.

FINALLY . . .

If all you really want is to come home from the theatre and eat some cold eggs and drink a glass of champagne, have your cook do this: Hard-boil some eggs, peel them, split them lengthwise, scoop out the yolks.

Then have her mix the yolks with an equal amount of *pâté de foie gras* and enough cream to make the thing workable, and then overstuff the eggs with it.

When you come home, have your butler set out the dish of eggs and open a bottle of champagne.

This, of all the recipes, is my personal favorite. Not so much the eggs, need I say, but that cook and butler.

For if I have learned one thing during the making of this book, it is this: Get a cook. No matter what the sacrifice involved: *Get a cook.*

Kitchens are all right to visit, but I wouldn't want to live there.

* *I N D E X* *